All in the golden afternoon Full leisurely we glide;
For both our oars, with little skill, By little arms are
While little hands make vain pretence Our wander

Ah, cruel Three! In such an hour, Beneath such
To beg a tale, of breath too weak To stir the tiniest
Yet what can one poor voice avail Against three

Imperious Prima flashes forth Her edict to "begin
In gentler tone Secunda hopes "There will be
While Tertia interrupts the tale Not *more* than once

Anon, to sudden silence won, In fancy they
The dream-child moving through a land Of wonders
In friendly chat with bird or beast— And half

And ever, as the story drained The wells of fancy
And faintly strove that weary one To put the
"The rest next time—" "It *is* next time!" The happy

Thus grew the tale of Wonderland: Thus slowly,
Its quaint events were hammered out— And now
And home we steer, a merry crew, Beneath the

Alice, a childish story take, And with a gentle
Lay it where childhood's dreams are twined. In
Like pilgrim's withered wreath of flowers Plucked

olied,
ngs to guide.

dreamy weather,
eather!

tongues together?

t"—

nonsense in it"—
a minute.

pursue
wild and new,

believe it true.

dry,

subject by,

voices cry.

one by one,
the tale is done,

setting sun.

hand

memory's mystic band,
n a far-off land.

The Art of Alice in Wonderland

Stephanie Lovett Stoffel

SMITHMARK

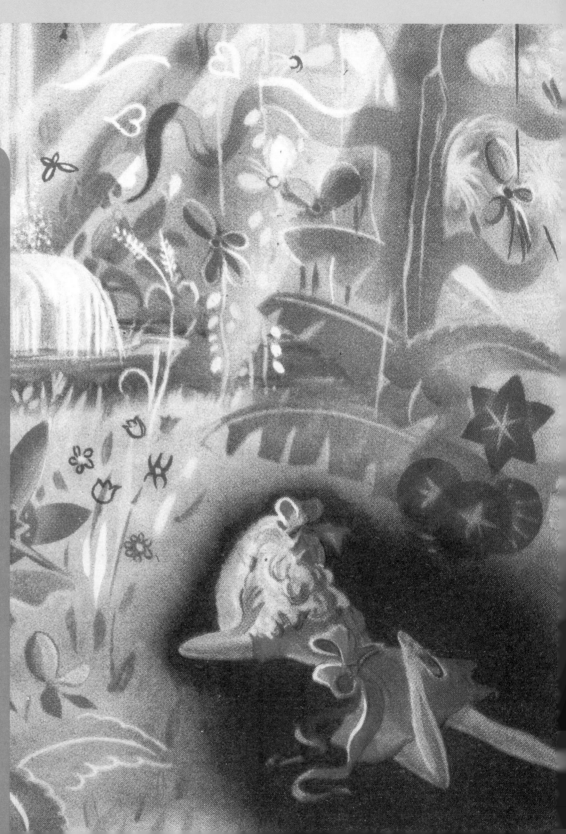

For Lucy My Child of Pure Unclouded Brow and Dreaming Eyes of Wonder

Library of Congress Cataloging-in-Publication Data

Stoffel, Stephanie Lovett, 1962–
      The art of Alice in Wonderland / by
    Stephanie Lovett Stoffel. — 1st Smithmark ed.
          p.   cm.
      Includes index.
      ISBN 0-7651-9133-4 (alk. paper)
      1. Carroll, Lewis, 1832–1898. Alice's
    adventures in wonderland—Illustrations.
    2. Carroll, Lewis, 1832–1898. Through the
    looking-glass—Illustrations. 3. Children's
    stories, English—Illustrations. 4. Fantastic
    fiction, English—Illustrations. 5. Alice
    (Fictitious character: Carroll) 6. Illustration
    of books—19th century. 7. Illustration of
    books—20th century.
I. Title.
PR4611.A73s76 1998   98-17605
823'.8—dc21   CIP

This edition published in 1998 by SMITHMARK
Publishers, a division of U.S. Media Holdings, Inc.,
115 West 18th Street, New York, NY 10011.

SMITHMARK books are available for bulk
purchase for sales promotion and premium use.
For details write or call the manager of special
sales, SMITHMARK Publishers, 115 West 18th
Street, New York, NY 10011

THE WONDERLAND
PRESS

Produced by The Wonderland Press, 160 Fifth
Avenue, Suite 723, New York, NY 10010

All illustrations and related items contained in this
book have been photographed from and are
courtesy of the Lovett Collection of Lewis Carroll
materials, Winston-Salem, North Carolina.

Editorial Director: Elizabeth Sullivan
Project Editor: Marisa Bulzone
Designers: Lynne Yeamans & Galen Smith

ISBN: 0-7651-9133-4

Printed in Hong Kong

10 9 8 7 6 5 4 3 2 1

Acknowledgments The author is indebted to W. John Campbell of The Wonderland Press for developing and nurturing this project; to Marisa Bulzone, editor, Lynne Yeamans and Galen Smith, designers, and to Marta Hallett and Elizabeth Sullivan at Smithmark. She is also grateful to Charles C. Lovett for help both tangible and intangible, and to Dr. Donald Rackin and C. K. Weigl, who generously and wisely critiqued the manuscript. Finally and always, she sends a garland of thanks to Lucy Lovett and Judge Stoffel.

Contents

A Story, the Truth, and a True Story

Curiouser and curiouser! If we live our lives with the slightest measure of thoughtful observation, every day we learn anew that the world is a stranger place than we had decided it was on the day before. People do and say things that make no sense to us, trying all the while to persuade us that they are being perfectly logical. Events swirl around us, revealing surprises and unlooked for conclusions, and sometimes mystifyingly dissipate, leaving us wondering what just happened and what it might mean.

Rightly so, when life is like this, we may well say that we feel like Alice in Wonderland. The sheer verisimilitude of Lewis Carroll's *Alice* books, *Alice's Adventures in Wonderland*

and *Through the Looking-Glass and What Alice Found There*, is one of the reasons they have been on everyone's bookshelf for over one hundred thirty years. On many a morning, the newspaper compares some political scene to the Mad Tea-party or comments that a new turn of events is sending us all down the rabbit hole. Opposing political candidates often appear in the papers as Tweedledum and Tweedledee, and at any given time, on any given newsstand, it's a sure bet that someone is saying that in modern life it takes all the running you can do just to stay in the same place.

This emotional recognition of Alice's truth isn't merely a British and American phenomenon. People may say that they feel like Alice, whether their native language is Japanese, Icelandic, Croatian, Africaans, Spanish, Turkish, Thai, Dutch, Hebrew, Serbian, Bengali, Lithuanian, Frisian, or one of more than seventy languages into which Alice has been translated. This is not merely a linguistic challenge or a novelty—people the world over have connected with

Alice. The stories and characters live in their minds, the many memorable quotes spring to their tongues, and the spirit of the tales becomes part of them.

How could this little tale, written by one particular person for another (a religious and intellectual young man for a bright and aristocratic child) at a very definite place and time (the idiosyncratic world of mid-19th-century Oxford) speak so much to so many for so long? As with any great piece of literature, the answer is both simple and complex, immediate and endless. Alice's story speaks of essential truths about the human condition, and it does so not in the blunt language of sociology or psychology but in the subtle tongue of art, leaving loose ends, dark corners, and mysterious twilights in which each reader sees his or her own personal meaning.

An achievement of this magnitude was not the original intention of the author. Charles Lutwidge Dodgson was merely trying to entertain some young friends on a lovely summer outing. At the time of the story's first telling, Dodgson was thirty years old and well on his way to becoming a successful academic, lecturing and tutoring in mathematics at Christ Church

College, Oxford. He was the son of a distinguished clergyman, and himself a deacon of the Church of England. Living in rooms at the college, he was far from his Yorkshire home, where he had been the oldest boy in a lively family of eleven children. Gifted with a lifelong flair for inventive games and storytelling, young Dodgson was happy to spend some of his leisure hours in a semblance of family life, taking children on picnics, playing parlor games, setting word puzzles for them, and spinning fantastic tales.

He had made special friends with the children of the new Dean of Christ Church, Henry George Liddell. In the first days of what was to be one of his principal avocations—photography—he met Alice Liddell in the Deanery garden and took a picture of her with her older sister Lorina. He had met Lorina and the oldest child, Harry, earlier, and was soon a fixture in their lives, tutoring Harry until he went away to school, and entertaining the girls. Their little sister Edith accompanied them in their outings once she was no longer a toddler. Together they made many an expedition, visiting the deer park at Magdalen College and the University Museum with its natural history wonders from around the world. The favorite treat to which they returned again and again, though, was renting a boat at Folly Bridge and rowing up- or downstream, enjoying a picnic before their return.

On July 4, 1862, Dodgson and another young clergyman of the university, Robinson Duckworth, collected the three girls for a river trip. Disappointed earlier that week by rain, the carefree party was now happy to be on the water at last. Duckworth was a great favorite with one and all, for he sang beautifully and shared in the rowing. Dodgson would later elegize that "golden afternoon" in the introductory poem to *Alice's Adventures in Wonderland*, describing the "dreamy weather" and the children clamoring for a tale. The oldest, Lorina, demanded that he "begin it"; Alice, the second, hoped "There [would] be nonsense in it"; and the youngest little girl interrupted "not *more* than once a minute."

In later years, those who were on this memorable trip would be asked to reminisce about it, and they recalled the sunshine, Dodgson extemporizing the story in response to the children's wishes, and Alice's insistence that he must write this one down for her. He began the next day, but it would be three years of expanding the story, laboring over his drawings, hiring a professional illustrator, seeking advice, and engaging a publisher before the story of "Alice in Wonderland" as we know it appeared. Dodgson did complete the hand-lettered and illustrated version that he had promised Alice, presenting it to her as *Alice's Adventures under Ground.* Sold by the widowed Alice in 1926, it fetched huge sums at two auctions and, after crossing the Atlantic twice, it now resides in the British Library on display. But there is a more convenient way to view it: Dodgson had it published in facsimile in 1886, and there are modern facsimile versions available today.

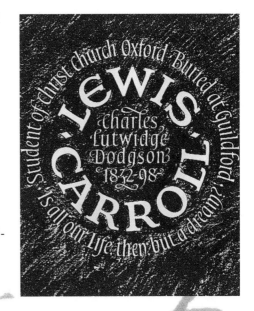

It is often said that Charles Dodgson adopted his pen name "Lewis Carroll" because a serious mathematician could not jeopardize his reputation publishing children's books. In fact, Dodgson had already begun publishing his poetry in periodicals, and he had first used the pen name in 1856, at age twenty-four, after writing his melancholy poem "Solitude." Even today, authors experience tremendous resistance from publishers and the public alike if they attempt to write in a genre other than what they are known for, as if their name were a trademark. Similarly, Dodgson wanted his real name to be associated with the academic publishing he intended to do in mathematics and logic, and so he chose another name for his literary efforts.

The editor who had accepted "Solitude" for *The Train* chose "Lewis Carroll" from a list that Dodgson had submitted—all of which were plays on his real name. He arrived at "Lewis Carroll" and "Louis Carroll" by reversing "Charles Lutwidge," Latinizing them, and returning them to English as their linguistic first cousins—a suitable method for an amateur magician whose name would become synonymous with the perplexities of mirror reversal, and certainly a more felicitous choice than the anagrams of his name, "Edgar Cuthwellis" and "Edgar U. C. Westhill."

One also reads anecdotes suggesting that Alice Liddell's manuscript version of the story was lying around and people happened to read it and then pressed the idea of publication upon the modest and surprised Mr. Dodgson. It is certainly true that he began writing out the story with no idea of publication, solely as a gift to the little girl who gave the heroine her name. However, long before he was able to complete his own illustrations and present the story to Alice, he had

Anon, to sudden silence

In fancy they pursue

The dream-child moving

Of wonders wild and new

In friendly chat with bir

And half believe it true.

won,

through a land

' or beast—

seen its potential and had begun to develop it for a wider audience. He asked advice of others, particularly family members of his friend, the noted fantasy writer George MacDonald. Their acclaim convinced him that he should give the tale not only to Alice but to the world.

To do so, Dodgson had to alter and expand the text considerably. *Alice's Adventures under Ground* is about half the length of *Alice's Adventures in Wonderland*. He removed or adapted parts of the story that were personal jokes and references among himself and the Liddell sisters, though much remains that springs directly from their friendship. For instance, the strange gathering on the banks of the Pool of Tears is a thinly disguised burlesque of an earlier river outing in which Duckworth, Dodgson, the girls, and Dodgson's Aunt Lucy and two of his sisters had all gotten soaked in a sudden rain shower. Duckworth is the Duck, Dodgson the Dodo, Lorina the Lory, and Edith the Eaglet. Likewise, the three little girls in the well in the Dormouse's tale are the sisters again: Elsie is Lorina Charlotte (L. C.), Lacie is an anagram of Alice, and Tillie was a nickname for Edith.

Dodgson's additions to *Alice under Ground* included two of the best-loved scenes, the Mad Tea-party and the encounter with the Cheshire Cat. The Duchess and the Queen of Hearts were developed from one original character, the Marchioness, which explains their sometimes confusing similarity. Martin Gardner's *The Annotated Alice* (New American Library, 1960) footnotes the references behind the text. After this seminal edition burst upon the scene, Gardner was so deluged with new information that he published *More Annotated Alice* (Random House, 1990) with completely new and different footnotes. Anyone interested in Alice would be richly rewarded by reading both.

Dodgson needed a publisher, and selected the distinguished house of Macmillan. Nineteenth-century publishing differed radically from the publishing scene of today. In place of the standard author-publisher contract, there were many different types of agreements between authors and publishers, including one-time leases of rights and various percentages of commissions. Dodgson presented his book to Alexander Macmillan, who responded that his firm was interested in having an involvement in the project. From that point on, Dodgson could be said to have co-published the book, retaining the right to make all the important decisions about the appearance of the book, and paying Macmillan's to print and distribute it under his direction. Macmillan's remained his publisher for some thirty years, and they enjoyed a personal and mutually beneficial relationship.

One of Charles Dodgson's defining and deeply personal characteristics was his longing to be an

The Dodo presents a Prize to Alice.

Alice's Adventures IN THE NEW WONDERLAND

The Yellowstone National Park

Walt Disney's Alice in Wonderland

ALICE'S RACE IN WONDERLAND

ADVENTURES OF ALICE IN WONDERLAND GAME

CHARLOTTE HENRY EDITION

MILTON BRADLEY COMPANY
SPRINGFIELD, MASSACHUSETTS
SPECIAL PERMISSION OF PARAMOUNT PRODUCTIONS INC.

artist. He became friends with a number of leading painters of his day, particularly those among the Pre-Raphaelite Brotherhood, and was a devoted gallery-goer. As a master art photographer, he was able to consider himself an artist, and rightly so: His work is much admired and studied today. Photography gave him the outlet he craved to express his visual aesthetic, and was very fulfilling and gratifying. Nevertheless, he still wanted badly to be able to draw well, to be an artist with a pencil. Though he sketched all his life, he was never satisfied with the results.

Dodgson understood that pictures are crucial to the success of a children's book. An experienced story-teller, he wasn't going to give children the kind of "boring" book Alice flees from, one with "no pictures or conversation." Children want action and dialogue, and Dodgson knew to leave the descriptions to a better medium than words—the illustrations. So when it came to preparing *Alice's Adventures in Wonderland* for publication, he realized that his own drawings would not do, and he looked for a professional illustrator. He secured an introduction to John Tenniel, leading political cartoonist for the humor weekly *Punch,* and the two undertook a partnership that

helped make *Alice* the marvel it is. Tenniel's matter-of-fact drawings give Dodgson's fantastical creatures the solidity and reality of this morning's newspaper. "Partnership" may not be quite the word, since Dodgson essentially art-directed his book and told Tenniel exactly what he wanted each picture to be like. However, he was respectful of Tenniel's opinions and took the older man's advice as well. This blending of talents created a seamless literary experience of word and image. In fact, Dodgson and Tenniel integrated verbal and visual information so entirely that it can be difficult to say which things we know about *Alice* from the text and which we know from the pictures. All in all, *Alice* would not have gotten the initial notice it did without the attention given to a new work by the well-known John Tenniel. Conversely, Tenniel would surely be chagrined to be best known today as the illustrator of *Alice in Wonderland.*

The book, in twelve chapters with forty-two illustrations, bound in attractive red cloth with gold stamping, came off the presses in the summer of 1865. Dodgson inscribed and sent out perhaps fifty copies, some specially bound in vellum, but was then obliged to ask for all of them back, since word came from John Tenniel that the

printing was faulty and must be redone. On at least some of those copies the ink appears to have been applied too heavily, causing the white areas in the pictures to be speckled with bleed-through from the other side. Dodgson agreed, and, still at his own expense, the book was entirely reprinted. He was to do this with other books of his that failed to come up to his standards, and his lifelong correspondence with Macmillan's is full of remonstrances that cost was never to outweigh his duty to give the public the very best product possible. The few surviving copies of the recalled books constitute the true first edition of an influential piece of Western literature, and have become almost impossible prizes in the rarefied heights of book collecting. The new copies of *Alice's Adventures in Wonderland* appeared in time for Christmas 1865, dated 1866. They sold well, and *Alice*'s popularity increased steadily, so that by the time *Through the Looking-Glass* appeared in 1872, an eager public awaited it.

Alice's international career began immediately, thanks to the rejected printing. Loathe to scrap entirely the sets of printed-but-never-bound sheets (1950 sets of them), Dodgson and Macmillan decided that they were good enough for the benighted colonies, and sold them to an American publisher. In fact, the U.S. edition appeared before the 1866 British first edition, and *Alice* was also pirated in the United States in magazines. Under Dodgson's supervision, a German translation appeared in 1869, and he quickly followed it with French and Italian. In the years since, the *Alice* books have been translated into more than seventy lan-

guages, with many different translations appearing in many of those languages. Their very difficulty, with the idiosyncratic language, puns, and poetry, seems to be a siren call to the translator. In fact, "Jabberwocky" has often been done as an exhibition piece for the sake of the challenge.

By the time *Alice's Adventures in Wonderland* was published, Dodgson was no longer so close with the Liddell children, who were growing into young women and whose mother discouraged an intimate relationship with a single man not qualified as a marriage prospect. However, his life was agreeably full of nieces and nephews, children of friends and colleagues, and children befriended at the seaside, with whom he continued his happy role

as jolly older brother. His own life was enriched with the love and intellectual challenge of children, and in return he gave many children the rare gift of the serious attention of an adult who genuinely connected with them as human beings. Whether or not he was ever in love with Alice Liddell herself, she seems to have become for him an icon of the child-friend, the prototype who was doubtless as bright and challenging as any little girl he had ever known, who prompted his great work, who inspired some of his best photography, and who was inevitably lost to him. Loss and melancholy were intertwined with the joy of being friends with children, for even though he often remained close with his child-friends after they were grown and parents themselves, their child-selves were gone forever. Children whom we love, we must always lose; the vanished child haunts us, and the presence of the adult does

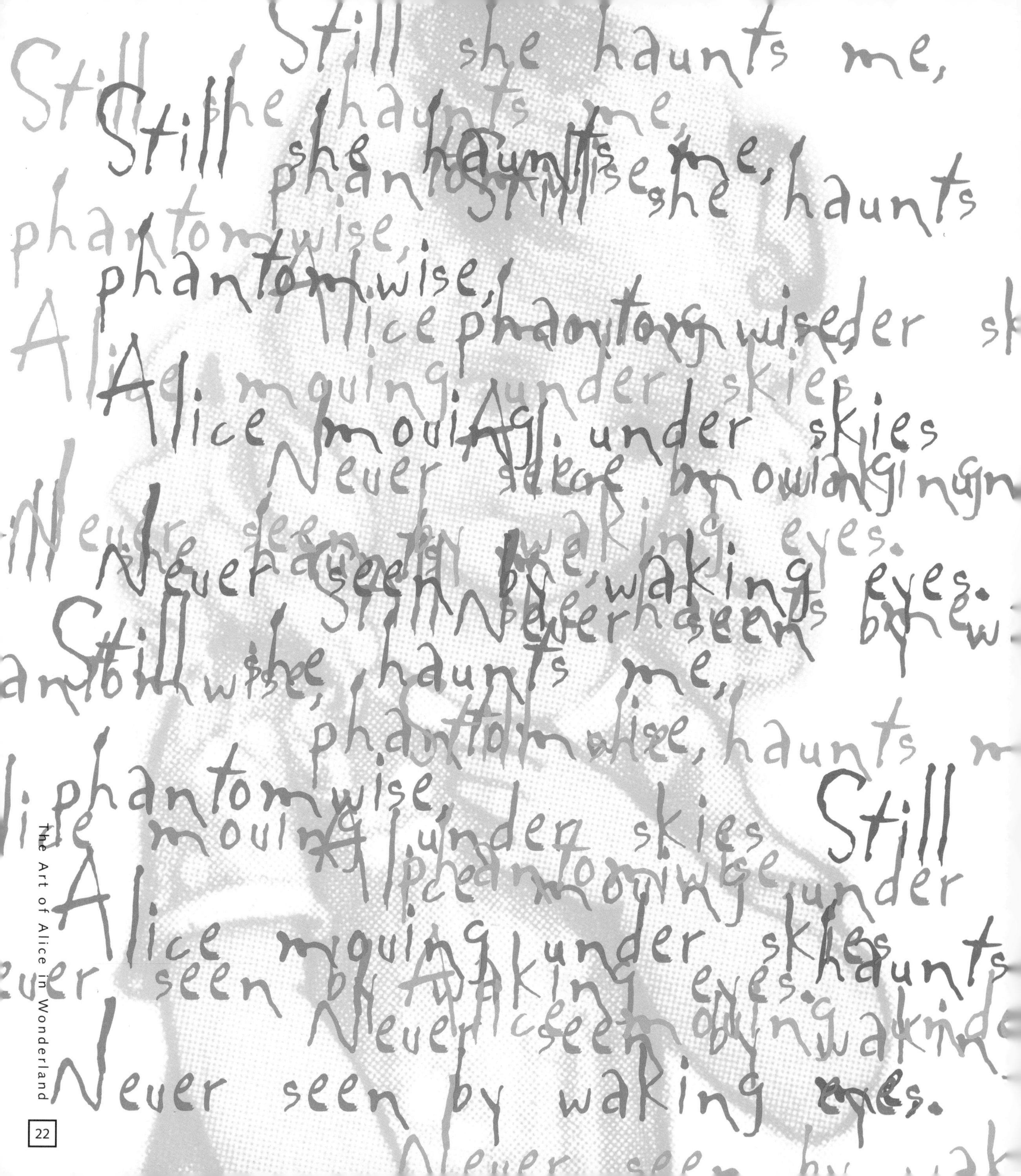

Still she haunts me,
phantomwise,
Alice moving under skies
Never seen by waking eyes.

Still she haunts me,
phantomwise,
Alice moving under skies
Never seen by waking eyes.

not keep us from listening for that skipping footstep, or from the pain of never hearing it.

Thus, *Through the Looking-Glass and What Alice Found There* was written not for any particular child-friend Dodgson had at the time, but seems inspired by the memory of Alice and by his awareness of the fleeting nature of youth. It sprang not from one occasion, but from a number of little stories and ideas, some dating back to his days of constantly seeing the Liddell children, some freshly developed with current child-friends. *Looking-Glass* notably contains Dodgson's own farewell to Alice as she leaves behind her childhood as well as him, in the person of the kindly and bumbling White Knight, to become a Queen. The book begins and ends with elegiac poems, looking back on happy summer days gone by, three children eagerly listening to a simple tale, but looking back from a present in which "Autumn frosts have slain July".

Still she haunts me, phantomwise,
Alice moving under skies
Never seen by waking eyes.

Alice haunts all of us, moving through her dreamworlds and ours. How this can be is a tantalizing question, and to try to answer it requires us to walk observantly and wonderingly through her dreamworlds ourselves. If we look and listen, the keys to the greatness of Lewis Carroll's work are there for us to find, and they open doors to reveal much about the ways literature has of speaking to us, the mind and heart of Lewis Carroll, and the nature and meaning of being human.

there and back again

The *Alice* books belong to a branch of literature that speaks deeply and clearly to the human psyche—stories of the journey. Journey literature uses the simple but powerful device of sending a character on a physical journey. On the road, that character can have adventures which provide opportunities for growth and development, and the journey also functions on a metaphorical level. The journeys we make in literature and life, from one stage of maturity and realization to another, can be frustratingly hard to detect. Journey literature brings that progress out from the subtle ether of personal interactions and people's interior life into a concrete, visible form.

The idea that a physical journey can be a way to

self-knowledge is not the province only of literature. It is sufficiently rooted in the human spirit as to appear in religions around the world. Taoism, one of the major spiritual practices of the East, is based on it; the word *Tao* actually means the Way. It emphasizes the idea that there is a right path for each of us to be taking through life, and that the best thing a person can do is to be attuned to the signs of one's own path. The purpose is not to be concerned with the journey's end, with goals and objectives, but only the process of living correctly so that we can follow the path that the universe intends for us—that is, to remain in harmony with who we are. There are adventures that each of us needs to have, and Taoism teaches us to find our own path in order to have the appropriate experiences and be in the right place at the right time.

In Christianity, Islam, and Shinto, a believer may be compelled to make a pilgrimage. A pilgrimage has a destination—Mecca, Canterbury, Compostella, Mount Fuji—but how one journeys on a pilgrimage is always as important as the shrine at the end. The process of overcoming hardships, of wearing prescribed garments, and of following a particular path

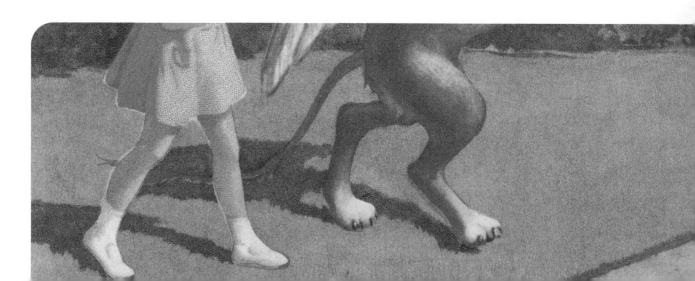

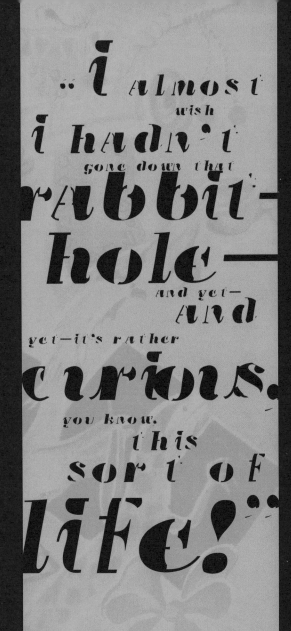

"..i almost wish i hadn't gone down that rabbit-hole—and yet—and yet—it's rather curious, you know, this sort of life!"

are all designed to transform the pilgrim into a different, renewed person at journey's end. Christians continue to observe the metaphorical pilgrimages of Lent and Advent, but since the physical journey to Lourdes or Jerusalem is so easily attainable these days—without the physical hardships and moral challenges of the trip—one doesn't necessarily feel any different when one gets there.

The central belief of Christianity is the incarnation of the deity as a

human being, and in that incarnation, Jesus said "I am the Way." Knowledge of Jesus is a journey that Christians are required to undertake in order to reach God. There are a number of tribal religions, including those among Native Americans and aboriginal Australians, that send young men on a journey so that they may return as full-fledged adults, ready to take their place in the society. However sophisticated and intellectual a culture

becomes, we all are physical beings, and we all readily understand and respond to the idea that we can accomplish things—difficult and monumental things—by doing something, by going somewhere. In one sense or another, none of us is where we want to be. If what we long for does not lie within us, then it must lie elsewhere—and a long road lies between.

In literature, we can look a long way behind us and find many tales of those who learn and grow on their voyages. Odysseus, in Homer's *Odyssey*, must face ten years of trials and obstacles before he can return to his wife Penelope. In the Arthurian legend of the knights of the Round Table, the Grail is located somewhere "out there," hidden so that Parsival and Lancelot must search for it, discovering themselves in the process. In the German epic poem, The *Nibelungenlied*, Siegfried kills the dragon in order to voyage to the underworld. In John Bunyan's prose allegory, *Pilgrim's Progress*, the Pilgrim makes his Progress, demonstrating how a non-allegorical Christian can overcome the obstacles on the road of life. Don Quixote travels the land on his own strange quest, from which perhaps his squire, Sancho Panza, and the reader learn more than Quixote himself. When civilized life gets to be too much to bear, Huck Finn lights out for the territories. Acquiring maturity was hardly his intention, but nevertheless in doing so he learns far more than he would have if he had stayed in school.

Journey literature has many layers, but its immediate appeal to the characters and to the reader is that it is engaging. Alice sets out through Wonderland and Looking-Glass Land not in order to learn and to grow by overcoming obstacles, but because she is curious and wants to have adventures. Journey literature stays alive and lively, read by people at different ages and stages of their lives, because it is exciting and entertaining.

We don't have to be English majors writing a term paper to want to read Huckleberry Finn. The journey of the hero is equally compelling to the reader.

As is often the case in life, Alice doesn't know what she's gotten herself into. Like any hero, she can't just have an adventure and return the same person as when she left. Adventures bring out facets of character the hero hadn't needed before; mettle gets tested and ingenuity taxed. Lessons wait on the road that are not to be found at home: In Tolkien's *The Hobbit*, or *There and Back Again*, Bilbo Baggins would rather stay in the Shire, but because of his reluctantly undertaken quest he becomes the transformed fellow, respected and loved, that we find at the end of the book.

Alice's adventures have many of the hallmarks of the traditional literary quest. She has a goal, which is to get to the beautiful gar-den or to the eighth square of the chess board. She meets strange beings who delay and dis-tract her, who threaten and test her. She must answer their questions, solve their riddles, appeal to them for help, and get away from them when they would keep her with them

forever. Her character is tested, and she remains polite and considerate, but still learns to use her ingenuity to avoid being trapped in a small episode that would keep her from realizing her larger goal. She has no fairy godmother, magic ring, or ruby slippers to help her, but she does manage to ask the right creature for help in Wonderland and gains the power to control her own size with the mushroom. In Looking-Glass Land, the only charm available to protect her is the advice the Red Queen gives her before the game begins: "Remember who you are!"

But *Alice in Wonderland* isn't just journey literature, any more than it sits neatly on the shelf of children's literature or satire. The *Alice* books aren't genre novels, but complex literature. Nevertheless, the powerful resonance of her journeys are part of the reason for Alice's fascinating grip on so many readers from so many diverse cultures. Lewis Carroll and the Cheshire Cat did not mean to reassure Alice that her amusing wanderings would result in her achieving something greater, but they do. Alice says that she doesn't much care which way she walks,

Therein lies the truth of the journey. The road goes ever on, in Tolkien's immortal words, and we all have faith deep in our bones that it will take us where we need to go, if only we keep walking long enough.

"—so long as i get somewhere." alice added as an explanation.

"oh, you're sure to do that," said the cat,

"if only you walk long enough."

alice says that she doesn't much care which way she walks,

figures of fun

Victorian England was a very adult place. Factories pumped out coal smoke, the bulk of the infamous London "fog." Rails clacked day and night with their loads of freight and passengers. Seafaring merchants brought the world's treasures to Britannia's doorstep and spread her virtues and customs to the four corners of the globe. The Great Exhibition of 1851 showcased imperial Great Britain's cultural and economic superiority. Working-class, middle-class, and aristocratic Britons were all satisfied that theirs was a prosperous, industrious nation, deservedly rewarded and destined for ever-greater achievements.

Running this enterprise was serious business, and people took themselves seriously. One felt a duty

to fulfill one's public and private roles, to be an informed citizen, and to raise the next generation to take their places in the great scheme of things. As was the freshly-mined ore to the finished steam engine, so was the unformed child to the mature British citizen. The nursery and the school were factories that manufactured empire-builders.

Lewis Carroll, however, as a friend of children, was well aware that they were far from being *tabulae rasae*, blank slates with no ideas of their own. With his own childhood alive within him and his nursery passport up to date, Carroll knew that even the most cooperative and eager-to-please child was the adult world's shrewdest critic.

The unsophisticated eyes of youth see clearly. The parent's self-image may be one of enormous success as an impressive authority figure, but the frank child sees the inconsistencies, the pomposity, the hypocrisy, and all the other human foibles all too plainly.

One of Lewis Carroll's child-friends later said of him, "We knew he was on our side, against the grown-ups." Children who have never met him know this, too, for the *Alice* books tell them so. Carroll wasn't spinning a fable to teach them to mind their manners or to be prudent or to remember the Golden Rule. He was telling them their own story, the story of a young person doing her best to manage in a strange world populated by capricious and not very sympathetic beings.

The storyteller seizes the young listener's confidence right away by speaking from Alice's point of view. She has become bored sitting with her older sister, who is reading a book that has no pictures

or conversations in it. The storyteller does not brand Alice as being bad or lazy because of her boredom; in fact, she is clearly more sensible than her sister in having no interest in such a dull book. It is her youthful curiosity—a trait at that time commonly painted as

leading to trouble in moral tales for children—that leads her away from the indifferent adult world to a magical adventure.

Throughout her journey, Alice encounters many characters who seem oddly familiar. They are the adults from her above-ground, waking life, transmogrified into absurd figures. Carroll has given his child-readers an invaluable gift, the chance to laugh safely at the foolishness they observe every day while making their way through the world. Not too far into the first book, Alice meets the Dodo. The Dodo bird does not seem to see himself as a helpless, pathetic, biological anachronism. Rather, the flightless and fluffy bird is pompous and self-important, and the Eaglet

mocks him for using long words that nobody understands. Alice struggles to maintain her composure as he solemnly presents her with her own thimble:

Then they all crowded round her once more, while the Dodo solemnly presented the thimble, saying, "We beg your acceptance of this elegant thimble"; and, when it had finished this short speech, they all cheered. Alice thought the whole thing very absurd, but they all looked so grave that she did not dare laugh, and as she could not think of anything to say, she simply bowed, and took the thimble, looking as solemn as she could.

This resembles the many meaningless ceremonies in which children bewilderedly participate to oblige adults. Their friend and ally, Lewis Carroll, lets them know that he understands how silly it all seems to them.

The March Hare and the Hatter make a two-against-one team, like parents at the dinner table. They criticize Alice's manners and grooming, and they quiz her pointlessly. The two have conversations that make sense between them but are

unintelligible to Alice, who puzzles over a remark that "seemed to her to have no sort of meaning in it, and yet it was certainly English." The tea party passes in a blur of patronizing rudeness and bizarre conversation, until Alice gives up on sitting politely in a social situation that excludes her. She gets up and walks away.

At the croquet ground, Alice must endure a particularly tedious type of adult. The Duchess reappears, in a more pleasant temper than she had been in at her own house, and promenades through the garden with Alice. As they walk, she completes every remark Alice makes with a moral. She grandly dispenses silly, nonsensical epigrams, going so far as to say that they are a present to Alice. Having to show gratitude for and be gracious about this kind of useless and obscure adult advice is surely one of the trials of youth, and Carroll invites his child-readers to laugh at the absurdity of adults trying to turn every incident in the day into a lesson:

"You're thinking about something, my dear, and that makes you forget to talk. I can't tell you just now what the moral of that is, but I shall remember it in a bit."

"Perhaps it hasn't one," Alice ventured to remark.

"Tut, tut, child!" said the Duchess. "Everything's got a moral, if only you can find it."

The Queen of Hearts can be more frightening than foolish. Constantly bellowing and enraged, she orders executions at any provocation. She has no other personality beyond her anger, and in fact Carroll later wrote that he imagined her as the

"you're thinking about something, my dear, and that makes you forget to talk. i can't tell you just now what the moral of that is, but i shall remember it in a bit."

"perhaps it hasn't one," alice ventured to remark.

"tut, tut, child!" said the duchess. "everything's got a moral, if only you can find it."

"embodiment of ungovernable passion—a blind and aimless Fury." Carroll knew that children all too often have to face adult anger, so he gave them a little wish fulfillment in the form of Alice's response to the Queen. The Queen is so extreme and outrageous, and her authority over Alice is so questionable, that Alice is able to face this oversized hot-air balloon and burst it by firmly yelling "Nonsense!" right back at her.

The Red Queen of *Through the Looking-Glass* is another overbearing monarch, but she is a different matter. Carroll later described her as "formal and strict, yet not unkindly; pedantic to the tenth degree, the concentrated essence of all governesses!" She crisply orders Alice to improve her deportment, scolds her for things said and unsaid, and tests her unmercifully on her knowledge of math, science, French, and other subjects. On their first meeting, Alice is in awe of the Queen and does her best to speak politely and to curtsy while she's thinking. After crossing the chess board, Alice becomes a Queen herself, and is more ready to argue; still, she is stymied by the Queen's peculiar command of logic. In the end, all she can do about the Red Queen is to seize the aggravating creature and shake her until she turns into a kitten.

Passing through the fourth square, Alice comes across the nursery rhyme characters Tweedledum and Tweedledee. It is clear that the brothers are supposed to be men, not boys, yet their behavior is extremely childish. Alice is much more mature than they, and even seems maternal in the way she speaks with them. She is grave and gentle as she helps them dress for their battle over the broken rattle, turning a laugh into a cough and being considerate of their feelings. Grown-ups can certainly quarrel fiercely over petty things, and Carroll hilariously lampoons the much-ado-about-nothing that every child has wondered at in his or her own home. Who cannot look back on some domestic scene and either smugly or ruefully (depending on whether one was the child or the adult involved) remember that the child was the only one behaving maturely?

The White Queen and the White King, whom Alice meets later on, are as laughably childish as the Tweedle brothers, but rather than being petty, they are simply helpless and dependent. The Queen cannot manage to dress herself without a maid, and she is benignly befuddled during the Red Queen's examination of Alice. The King, nervously watching the Lion and the Unicorn battle for the crown, is dependent upon his two Messengers. His speech is naively literal, and his possession of the crown seems tenuous at best. Alice is commendably gentle with these two, and the reader smiles with her at these childlike monarchs.

An altogether less agreeable, but enormously entertaining, character is the memorable Humpty Dumpty. From his perch on high, he haughtily hands down his pronouncements, with no regard for Alice's opinions or feelings. A more self-centered and self-satisfied being would be hard to imagine. Despite his phenomenal abruptness and rudeness to Alice, she makes an effort not to laugh at his grandiose announcement of the King's promise of a rescue should he fall, and she refrains from pointing out his complete inability to perform mathematical subtraction. He, on the other hand, has no compunctions at all about disagreeing with her, and is pleasant only when she asks questions and lets him talk. The pontificating adult who bulldozes the child, turning a conversation into a monologue, is an all-too-familiar figure.

Carroll does not spare himself in his catalogue of adult follies. Alice is rescued from the Red Knight and escorted through the next-to-last square by the kindly White Knight. With his mind always at work on ideas and inventions, the naive White Knight is quite unable to manage ordinary activities. His otherworldly remoteness and physical ineptitude make him one of the most comical characters in either of the *Alice* books, an absent-minded professor whose life is a series of pratfalls. The scene is sweetly elegiac as well, for this is Carroll's sketch of himself as the gentle, foolish old protector of young girls, who perhaps can take perfectly good care of themselves and are simply being kind to walk with him a while.

For adult readers, seeing our foibles so neatly and hilariously skewered is guaranteed to bring on a case of combined giggles and blushes—unless of course, one is of the Humpty Dumpty type and entirely blind to the possibility of having foibles. Furthermore, even grown-ups must deal with authority figures of many different stripes. We can take just as much naughty pleasure as children do in recognizing Alice's companions. Teachers, bosses, relatives, co-workers, government officials, little Caesars, and loving parents—they are all there, the archetypes of all our lives, caught on candid camera. The vivid truthfulness that infuses the characters makes the comedy that much more successful and keeps them vibrantly alive through the generations.

Webs of Words

Although Lewis Carroll worked as a professional mathematician, he was heart and soul a logician. Thinking clearly and correctly evaluating statements was of the utmost importance to him. To understand that he independently weighed every issue in his life, rather than embracing any ideology, reveals the bedrock of his character and motivations. His mission to help others to do the same, to have that kind of integrity and not to be misled by persuasive but faulty arguments, drove him to bring logic out of the academy: His final, though uncompleted, work was a logic book designed to give general readers the tools to think for themselves.

His familiarity with the workings of logic made

"What do you mean by that?" said the Caterpillar sternly. "Explain yourself!"

"I can't explain *myself*, I'm afraid, sir," said Alice, "because I'm not myself, you see."

"I don't see," said the Caterpillar.

Carroll keenly aware that words are imprecise. Ambiguity in the words themselves and the peculiarities of everyday usage make the application of regular laws to verbal statements maddening. While numbers "behave" themselves when used in mathematical operations, words can twist and turn the meaning of an idea. The ability of words to cloak meaning at the same time as they purport to convey this very meaning is what makes logic such a fascination and challenge. It also can cause humorous misunderstandings and comical manipulations of meaning. Carroll constantly plays with words and meaning throughout the *Alice* books, in narrative asides as well as in the dialogue. The extraordinary rightness of his language is in large part responsible for the power of the books to endure in one's mind and in entire cultures.

Alice finds herself in many frustrating conversations—which are entertaining for the reader—because the characters insist on using language literally. They respond to the actual meaning of the words, but ignore the conventional understanding and unspoken communications of ordinary conversation. In Wonderland, Alice and the reader both learn that without shared assumptions, people cannot communicate. For example, when Alice speaks to the Caterpillar, she uses polite

rhetorical questions, which he then answers briefly and truthfully:

"What do you mean by that?" said the Catepillar sternly.

"Explain yourself."

"I can't explain *myself* I'm afraid, sir," said Alice,

"because I'm not myself, you see."

"I don't see," said the Catepillar.

His way of responding precisely and abruptly to whatever she says makes him an extremely rude conversationalist; the narrator tells us that Alice has never been so much contradicted in all her life. Because the Caterpillar is not interested in using words to establish rapport, he refuses to participate in simple social rituals such as agreeing with someone for the sake of the conversation. Alice explains that:

"Being so many different sizes in a day is very confusing."

"It isn't," said the Catepillar.

Eventually, Alice decides that there is no use in talking to the Duchess's Frog Footman, who ignores the unspoken communication that Alice's knock on the door means she wants to get in. He tells her in great

"Being so many different sizes in a day is very confusing."

"It isn't," said the Caterpillar.

detail why it is of no use knocking. When Alice finally verbalizes her desire to get in, twice, he simply asks if she is to get in at all, and in answer to her plea "But what am I to do?" tells her she may do anything she likes. While this is indubitably true, it isn't at all helpful. Another literal-minded Frog at another door, toward the end of *Through the Looking-Glass*, is also prevented—by semantics—from helping her get through the door. She wants someone to answer the door, so of course he wants to know what the door has been asking!

Alice has a particularly dysfunctional conversation with the Cheshire Cat. She assumes he will understand what it is she really wants to know, while he answers the questions she actually asks. Wanting advice on what would be the safest and most interesting places to visit, she asks the Cat which way she ought to walk. "'That depends a great deal on where you want to get to,' said the Cat." He assures her that she will get somewhere if only she walks long enough, and she gives up and changes the subject. She continues to get trapped by entirely mistaken statements with which she just can't argue:

"There's nothing like eating hay when you're faint," [the White King] remarked to her, as he munched away. "I should think throwing cold water over you would be better," Alice suggested: "or some sal-volatile." "I didn't say there was nothing _better_," the King replied. "I said there was nothing like it."

Of all the troublesome talkers Alice meets, Humpty Dumpty is the true master of words and their power to entrap. He says:

"How old did you say you were?"

Alice made a short calculation, and said "Seven years and six months."

"Wrong!" Humpty Dumpty exclaimed triumphantly.

"You never said a word like it!"

"I thought you meant 'How old are you?'" Alice explained.

"If I'd meant that, I'd have said it," said Humpty Dumpty.

Most of the creatures that Alice meets don't seem to be difficult on purpose. It's just that they apparently can't help taking language literally. Humpty Dumpty, however, deliberately controls communication by using words to mean whatever he chooses, and he is contemptuous of Alice for being the straight man to his pronouncements. By not using the conventional meanings of words, he forces whomever he is talking to into a subordinate position. Once Alice has been humbled and stops acting like an equal partner in the conversation, he is much more congenial. She asks him what he means by the word "impenetrability":

"Now you talk like a reasonable child," said Humpty Dumpty, looking very much pleased. "I meant by 'impenetrability' that we've had enough of that subject, and it would be just as well if you'd mention what you mean to do next, as I suppose you don't mean to stop here all the rest of your life."

When she is finally dismissed by Humpty Dumpty, Alice marches off, saying to herself "of all the unsatisfactory people I ever met," taking comfort in using such a long, grand word. She is certainly using it correctly, for it is an excellent word to describe trying to talk to someone who communicates entirely with and on his own terms.

Carroll entertains the reader and perplexes Alice with other kinds of word play, too. One of the first lessons in logic is the syllogism, a series of statements and a conclusion that is a basic tool for determining whether an argument truly proves a conclusion. For example: All hippopotamuses are blue, and George is a hippopotamus. Therefore, George is blue. When Alice is defending herself from the Pigeon's accusations that she is trying to steal eggs, she has the wind taken out of her sails by a faulty syllogism proposed by the Pigeon:

Serpents eat eggs, and girls eat eggs. Therefore,

Alice doesn't actually believe this, but it does give her pause, as does the Cheshire Cat's pseudo-logical argument that proves he's mad. She accepts the premise that a dog's not mad:

"Well then," the Cat went on, "you see a dog growls when it's angry, and wags its tail when it's pleased. Now I growl when I'm pleased, and wag my tail when I'm angry. Therefore I'm mad."

Furthermore, the Cat proves to Alice that she is mad as well, through another syllogism that is hard to refute, because it's logically correct:

"Everyone here is mad, and you're here. Therefore, you're mad."

Comical slips in logic pepper the story. We don't need to know the formal term, begging the question, for this fallacy to know that the Queen of Hearts has made a roundabout and meaningless definition of the Mock Turtle in saying it's the thing from which Mock Turtle Soup is made. Alice is exasperated when, at the trial, the King decides that the Knave's guilt is proven by the fact that the verses in evidence are not in his handwriting and not signed by him—for if his intentions were good he wouldn't have

girls are ♡ serpents.

disguised his writing and he would have signed the verses. How can the White Queen be correct in saying that when the rule is "jam every other day," one never gets jam because each day is today? When exactly is a day an "other" day? Alice and the reader pause to put a finger on just what is wrong with the Hare and Hatter's use of the word "more":

> "Take some more tea," the March Hare said to Alice, very earnestly.
>
> "I've had nothing yet," Alice replied in an offended tone, "so I can't take more."
>
> "You mean you can't take <u>less</u>," said the Hatter: "it's very easy to take <u>more</u> than nothing."

When the Cheshire Cat partially materializes on the croquet ground, the Queen of Hearts issues her standard command of "Off with his head!" This throws the King of Hearts and the executioner into a fine semantic argument that teeters along the knife edge of what the meaning of words has to do with the reality they are supposed to describe. The executioner refuses to proceed because a head cannot be cut off unless there is a body to cut it off from, while the King maintains that anything that has a head can be beheaded. They become completely stymied in defining beheading, in a manner not unlike the question of whether a tree falling makes a sound if no one is there to hear it.

Carroll makes another little joke on the power of words to obscure their own meaning when he has the Duchess rephrase the direct and admirable moral "Be what you would seem to be" as "Never imagine yourself not to be otherwise than what it might appear to others that what you were or might have been was not otherwise than what you had been would have appeared to them to be otherwise." As Peter Heath points out in *The Philosopher's Alice* (St. Martin's Press, 1982), the restatement is a paradox, because its obscurity violates the very moral it expresses.

Puns abound, such as the very simple ones of the Mouse trying to dry the Pool of Tears creatures by reciting a very dry history lesson, or Alice's belief that the Mouse's Tale is his tail. One of the Duchess's morals is a pun on the British maxim on frugality: "Take care of the pence, and the pounds will take care of themselves," and is also, inadvertently on her part, about puns as well: "Take care of the sense, and the sounds will take care of themselves." Carroll conjures up some amusing images, such as suppressing the guinea pigs in the trial scene by stuffing them into sacks, and he makes the most of this type of word play. The subjects which the Gryphon and Mock Turtle studied in school are funny, but they are also evocative and enchanting: The pair had lessons in the branches of mathematics—Ambition, Distraction, Uglification, and Derision—and in Mystery, ancient and modern; Drawling, Stretching, Fainting in Coils from the art teacher; and the two classical languages, Laughing and Grief. They stir in the mind a suggestion of layers of meaning; puns, yes, but also poetry.

The tricky thing about logic is that it addresses the truth of an argument, regardless of the truth of the terms in which the argument is expressed. In the formal study of logic, we can use symbols to see clearly the mechanism of the argument, but in ordinary life it is easy to be distracted by whether we believe the original premise or the conclusion—and consequently to lose track of whether the argument really proves anything. The

truth of the words and the truth of the logical structure are not the same thing. For example, the March Hare tells Alice that she should say what she means:

> "I do," Alice hastily replied; "at least—at least I mean what I say—that's the same thing, you know."
>
> "Not the same thing a bit!" said the Hatter. "Why, you might just as well say that 'I see what I eat' is the same thing as 'I eat what I see'!"
>
> "You might just as well say," added the March Hare, "that 'I like what I get' is the same thing as 'I get what I like'!"
>
> "You might just as well say," added the Dormouse, who seemed to be talking in his sleep, "that 'I breathe when I sleep' is the same thing as 'I sleep when I breathe'!"
>
> "It *is* the same thing with you," said the Hatter....

"Have you guessed the riddle yet?" the Hatter said, turning to Alice again.

"No, I give it up," Alice replied: "what's the answer?"

"I haven't the slightest idea," said the Hatter.

"Nor I," said the March Hare.

Alice sighed wearily. "I think you might do something better with the time," she said, "than wasting it in asking riddles that have no answers."

Does "I x what I y" equal "I y what I x?" Alice thinks so, but then the Hatter and Hare demonstrate through powerful examples that the two statements don't mean the same thing at all. Then the Dormouse undermines their proof with an example in which the statements are equivalent. Even though the Hatter and Hare correctly maintain that the two statements don't say the same thing, they are wrong to think they can definitively prove it by offering examples, as Alice sees when the Dormouse confounds them. Contemplating the kaleido- scope of words and meaning, we are left to wonder whether it is even possible to say what we mean or mean what we say. French critics in particular have admired Lewis Carroll's writing for its affinity with the theater of the absurd. Alice might well be walking from one Ionesco play to another as she passes into each scene, populat- ed by characters so immersed in their own versions of reality that they do not even have the ability to communicate with someone who doesn't share their frame of reference. In dealing with the Duchess, the Tea-party, the trial, the Tweedles, the Old Sheep, the banquet in her honor, and so on, Alice makes a sincere attempt to break through and talk with the characters. When it evolves that the only way to interact with them is to be manipulated by them and subordinate her own identity to their peculiar reality, she does the only sane thing: Rather than assuming she is obliged to fit in or mistaking others' choices for some defini- tive way to live, she walks away: "It's the stupidest tea- party I ever was at in all my life!"

The Tulgey Wood

As Maurice Sendak likes to point out, there isn't really such a thing as good children's literature—there is only good literature. If it's intended for children, good literature must still have all the qualities it would have if written for adults. The *Alice* books are clever and witty, inventive and amusing, and everyone enjoys them for those virtues. In fact, there are many, many abridged editions for very young readers that tell a story that bounds giddily from scene to scene, with bright, perky pictures, making the story nothing more than a charming adventure.

Charming it may be, but *Alice* would not still be with us solely on the merits of funny characters and strange adventures. As literature, the *Alice* books

"THE BLUE OF HEAVEN IS LARGER THAN THE CLOUD"
— Browning

Alice's Adventures in Atomland
in the Plastic Age

By
RICHARD M. FIELD

approach the depth and breadth of the human experience by touching on many serious concerns we have about our existence and our place in the world. They also respect the child-reader enough not to pretend that life is always safe and sunny. Children know that there are monsters in the closet and a terrible insecurity in the daylight world, and *Alice* would not be of such interest to them or to adults if it ignored our anxieties.

Traditional fairy tales speak to successive generations because they address essential fears and usually show innocent children triumphing over those who would victimize them. *Hansel and Gretel* and similar folktales involve children who have been abandoned or even deliberately betrayed by those they trust to protect them—their parents. They are nearly eaten by the evil that preys on unprotected children before they are able to save themselves through their own ingenuity. Cinderella's father is unable to stop her from being made a slave in her own home, and while her own goodness wins her supernatural aid, she suffers until she is able to prove her identity. The original tale violently makes visible a family's dysfunctions so that we can at any age understand lessons that would be more subtle in real life. Even the cleaned-up Disney version of *Cinderella* is a horrible parable of the cat-eat-mouse world that a child's family life can be.

Enduring stories don't always turn out well at all. Unlike the red-headed Princess Ariel, Hans Christian Andersen's Little Mermaid doesn't win her bet with the sea witch. As the sun sets on the third day, she feels her body become sea foam. Yet, there is comfort in the order of the world, for the daughters of the air, impressed with her fidelity, take her to become one of them in an ethereal life which neither the mermaid nor the sea witch had imagined for her. Comfort can be cold indeed—the Little Match Girl joins her grandmother in heaven, her body found frozen in a doorway. It's heart-breaking, but how much more awful if children could find no acknowledgment that suffering and death exist, and that they might have some meaning we cannot fathom in this world. And how much safer and more gentle to incorporate some of the harsher

moments of life through the mediation of the story, where we can feel and know a truth without having to learn everything the hard way. When literature lives up to its duty and isn't afraid to tell the truth, children whose lives are safe and happy can begin to understand the larger world, and children who lead tragic lives may find an unexpected helping hand in a lonely search for meaning.

So Lewis Carroll, ever knowledgeable about the inner life of children, playfully and fearlessly incorporated the dark side of life into his works, making the *Alice* books far less whimsical than they may appear. Alice isn't even all the way down the rabbit hole when Carroll mentions that she doesn't want to drop the marmalade jar for fear of killing somebody underneath, a straightforward but startling concern for a seven-year-old. The first death joke appears in the next paragraph: Alice is congratulating herself on how brave they will think her at home, since any falls will seem nothing after this one. She says, "'Why I wouldn't say anything about it, even if I fell off the top of the house!' (Which was very likely true.)" The narrator is winking at his child-readers, at Alice's expense.

As Alice considers the wisdom of taking the "Drink Me" bottle at its word, she recalls a number of cautionary tales she has read about the disasters that can befall careless children. In a whimsically understated passage, the narrator lists

some of these catastrophes: "…she had read several nice little stories about children who had got burnt, and eaten up by wild beasts and other unpleasant things, all because they *would* not remember the simple rules their friends had taught them; such as, that a red-hot poker will burn you if you hold it too long; and that if you cut your finger *very* deeply with a knife, it usually bleeds; and she had never forgotten that, if you drink much from a bottle marked "poison," it is almost certain to disagree with you, sooner or later."

As the bottle is not marked "poison," Alice drinks it, very undeservedly escaping poisoning.

What the bottle does rather than disagree with her is cause her to shrink to ten-inches high. Waiting to see if she will shrink any further, Alice worries that she might go out like a candle. "'I wonder what I should be like then?' And she tried to fancy what the flame of a candle looks like after the candle is blown out." This existential concern comes up again in *Through the Looking-Glass*, when Tweedledum tells her that the Red King is dreaming her and that if he were to wake up, she would go out like a candle. Like the riddle about where someone's lap goes when they stand up, the threat of being a candle flame that has gone out can be dismissed as a semantic trick and certainly explained factually, but it is also a darkly fascinating thing to contemplate the nature of something that only exits in certain circumstances. It is disturbing to wonder about a type of existence that isn't absolute, but depends on other conditions. What would the flame of a candle be like when it's been blown out? And what would happen if human existence were like that?

We take a peek at another grim reality, the unfortunate and inescapable truth that what is good for one may be deadly for another—the eat-or-be-eaten principle that lurks behind our more civilized ideas. When Alice is in the Pool of Tears, she repeatedly offends the mouse, and later the birds and other creatures on the shore, by singing the praises of nice pet animals who have soft fur and do tricks, and who also catch and kill mice, rats, and birds. It is a startling and sobering contrast to consider how sweet, normal, and beneficial Dinah the cat and the neighbor's terrier are to Alice and to us, yet how deadly and terrible they are to the creatures Alice is talking with. The creatures in the story are humanized, but apparently they live genuine animal lives; the tail/tale the Mouse tells to explain his horror of cats and dogs is a grim picture of life on the bottom of the food chain.

Another of the unhappy facts of life avoided by shallow children's books is violence. Alice copes with some frightening violence, made more nightmarish by the matter-of-fact attitudes of the characters. In the Duchess's kitchen, fire irons, pots, and plates are hurled at the Duchess and the baby, hitting them too, and the Duchess's speech and behavior are described several times as being violent. She

orders Alice to be beheaded, as does the Queen of Hearts. Alice marvels at the number of executions the Queen orders: "They're dreadfully fond of beheading people here: the great wonder is, that there's anyone left alive!" The Queen of Hearts is blind anger personified, and she would be truly terrifying if Alice were vulnerable to her. However, since Alice is not in her power, and knows it, Carroll uses the Queen as a means to look at and experience the dangers of ungoverned human rage. Moreover, there is a lot of noisy fighting and uproar in *Through the Looking-Glass* that Alice is described as being alarmed by. The quarreling Tweedle brothers prepare for a battle; the King's four thousand, two hundred, and seven horses and men crash through the woods to rescue Humpty Dumpty; the Lion and the Unicorn are drummed out of town in a fashion that sends Alice to her knees with her hands over her ears; and the Red and White Knights furiously duel over her.

Early on in *Through the Looking-Glass*, Alice comes across the poem "Jabberwocky," which sets a disturbing tone for the book. It is unclear to Alice as well as the reader exactly what this poem is about, but some kind of monster that whiffles and burbles threatens a boy and is killed by him. As Alice says, "Somehow it seems to fill my head with ideas—only I don't exactly know what they are!"—a sentiment that aptly describes the provocative effect of the *Alice* books themselves. Literature that is enduring and that offers meaning to generations of readers tends not to be literature with brightly-lit corners and neat explanations. If we could tidily explain *Hamlet*, it wouldn't be a very interesting play, and if there were simple answers to the questions raised in *Alice*, it would sit on the shelf next to Beatrix Potter's *Tales of Peter Rabbit* rather than with James Joyce's *Ulysses* and other literature that fills our heads with half-seen ideas.

Carroll actually planned to use the illustration of the Jabber-wock as the frontispiece for *Through the Looking-Glass*, setting the keynote for the story. After consulting with a number of mothers on how frightening they thought it would be to children, he decided to tuck it into the body of the story and to begin the book instead with Alice and the White Knight. "Jabberwocky" recurs in the tale when Alice asks Humpty Dumpty about it, and its haunting cadences make it one of the most quoted and translated pieces Carroll ever wrote. No one knows what it really *means*, but every-one loves reciting it. "Chortle" (a combination of "chuckle" and "snort") and "galumph" are Carrollisms that made their debut in the poem and that can now be found in any English dictionary. Somehow, "Jabberwocky" sits there in the back of our imagina-tions, under a mental rock, and teases us to plumb its depths.

Carroll does not hesitate to provoke the imagination with some scary concepts. Periodically, and inconsistently, he brings into the story of *Looking-Glass* some of the oddities created by living in a mirror universe. For instance, Alice must walk away from the Red Queen in order to go toward her, and the White Queen screams before she pricks her finger. Some of the aspects of backward living are threaten-ing and dangerous to someone from our side of the mirror. It's one thing to have to learn new rules of communication, calling things by their opposites ("When you say hill," the Queen interrupted, "*I* could show you hills, in comparison with which you'd call that a valley."), but it can be deadly to get the opposite of what you need. When Alice has been made exhausted and thirsty by running alongside the Red Queen, the Queen gives her a dry cracker to quench her thirst.

"Somehow it seems to fill my head with ideas—only I don't exactly know what they are!"

One might well feel a little desperate to find oneself trapped in a land where by definition one cannot get water when thirsty. Another alarming undercurrent is created when the White Queen explains that the King's messenger, Hatta, is in prison being punished; the trial doesn't begin until Wednesday, and the crime comes after that. Alice wants to know what would happen if he never commits the crime, and the Queen proves by some verbal sleight of hand that that would be better still. Alice protests and is trying to pinpoint the mistake when she is cut off. This is a very upsetting kind of determinism for those of us who live in a forward flow of time. It's a nightmare world indeed if everything we do is known by everyone else and we suffer the consequences of our future actions even if we decide later not to do them.

Some of the nightmare quality of the *Alice* books depends on the choices made by the illustrator of the particular edition at hand. Since Carroll described next to nothing about the appearance of the characters or scenes, realizing his visual conceptions through his work with Tenniel, subsequent illustrators have had enormous latitude to interpret the story. He or she may choose to make the characters cute and friendly, the colors bright and cheerful, the atmosphere sunny and light. Contrariwise, as Tweedledee would say, the illustrator can make the most of the characters' outlandishness and of Alice's vulnerability. There is a huge potential for grotesquerie in the creatures of Wonderland and Looking-Glass Land, which Arthur Rackham, for instance, played up in his classic illustrations. He shows us what the face of a human-sized rabbit would actually be like; his Hatter is a disturbing, elfin being, and the landscape of his Wonderland is gray and blighted. The strength of Tenniel's illustration was the grotesques and caricatures he drew weekly for the satirical humor magazine, *Punch*: His straight-faced rendering of them gives the stories the peculiar reality of a dream, in which the outrageous seems perfectly normal.

The artist's treatment of Alice also has a great effect on how menacing we find the other characters to be. If she calmly or even happily interacts with them, that tells the reader that the characters are not to be feared, however strange they appear. The great contemporary illustrator Barry Moser chose to have the reader experience Alice's dreams through her eyes. Even though his woodcut illustrations are primarily portraits rather than narrative scenes, they are among the most alarming, because without the mediation of Alice, we are left on our own with the characters confronting us directly.

Both tales end in a nightmarish disintegration of Alice's surroundings. The Wonderland trial makes less and less sense and the King and Queen become more threatening toward Alice, until finally everything blows up around her. Alice's banquet at the end of *Through the Looking-Glass* is even more bizarre, with candles growing to the ceiling, bottles flying around the room, and the White Queen disappearing into the soup. There is a sense of ominous emergency:

instead of the Queen, there was the leg of mutton sitting in the chair. "Here I am!" cried a voice from the souptureen, and Alice turned again, just in time to see the Queen's broad good-natured face grinning at her for a moment over the edge of the tureen, before she disappeared into the soup.

There was not a moment to be lost. Already several of the guests were lying down in the dishes, and the soup-ladle was walking up the table towards Alice's chair, and beckoning to her impatiently to get out of its way.

These panicked moments of total chaos tap a primal fear of loss of control without even a frame of reference. Things can indeed fall apart completely, leaving us to our own devices. How Alice manages in the face of this very basic catastrophe we will see later. First, let us bravely consider a human quality that Carroll knew human beings are terribly anxious about—one that is difficult to talk about concretely, that has been the crux of myriad schools of philosophy, and that he prods us to turn over and over in both *Alice* books: namely, our identity.

chapter six

Around the world and through the ages, myths and stories have helped humankind wrestle with one of our most disturbing issues—identity. Who are we? and how are we different from each other? We comment wryly on not being the same person we were in our youth, but then, what if we truly are *not* the same person? What makes a person an individual, and how do we hang on to that?

These issues are slippery and abstract. It's hard to talk about the sense of self, for the self lives invisibly and acts mysteriously. On the inside, no person has brown eyes or a funny nose or any other characteristic we can all look at and agree on. We can describe ourselves as the sort of person who

chooses to act in certain ways, but it is a notorious snarl in the human condition that people constantly do things that are "out of character." Tolstoy gave up on the idea that people have special, particular qualities, and instead suggested that people are like rivers: As the same river is broad and shallow in one place, deep and fast in another, cold here and warm there, so too does each individual contain the possibilities for all human qualities, capable of being in different places and at different times generous, cruel, dependent, powerful, and so on. Fair enough, but if someone's actions and the qualities that we believe caused those actions fail to define him or her, then we are left with little we can see that keeps *me* from being *you*.

One of the things that enables the *Alice* books to haunt the imagination is that they continually tap into our anxiety about our identity. Whatever elements are changed when the books are made into a movie or play, whatever splendid pieces of the Mad Tea-party are replaced with second-rate jokes, there remains Carroll's imperious Caterpillar, puffing smoke and sternly asking "Who are *you*?"

Alice is unable to explain or identify herself to him. Her loss of identity had begun in the hall of doors after her second change of size. At that early moment in the book, her reaction to everything being so different is to wonder if she herself is no longer the same person that she was the day before she changed sizes: "But if I'm not the same, the next question is, Who in the world am I? Ah, *that's* the great puzzle!"

It certainly is—for all of us. In Alice's case, it means wondering if she's been changed into anyone else she knows.

When Alice puts her theory to the test and finds she cannot remember her lessons, she cries upon proving that she must be Mabel after all. Readers are meant to be amused at her misguided criteria for identifying herself, yet we are also meant to wonder if we could come up with a better way.

At the beginning of her adventures, Alice

> "I'm sure I'm not Ada," she said, "for her hair goes in such long ringlets, and mine doesn't go in ringlets at all; and I'm sure I can't be Mabel, for I know all sorts of things, and she, oh! she knows such a very little! Besides, she's she, and I'm I, and oh dear, how puzzling it all is!"

imagines that "they" (i.e., adults above-ground) will put their heads down the rabbit hole and call her to come up again. She resolves to say, "Who am I then? Tell me that first, and then, if I like being that person, I'll come up: if not I'll stay down here till I'm somebody else." Alice realizes that she is changing, and her reaction is to plan to stay underground until she likes who she is—a remarkable decision that is more or less what eventually happens.

Alice's perception that she is no longer herself springs partly from the peculiar nature of her adventures and partly from her changes in size. It would be an over-simplification to say that the story is a metaphor for growing up, but Alice's disorientation over her changes in size irresistibly suggests that the growing process precipitates an identity crisis. Certainly in real life, awareness of changes in one's physical self goes hand-in-hand with anxiety about who one is. Being a child is part of a child's identity, and if childhood is being stripped away, then the adolescent is forced, sometimes urgently, to find someone new to be. Carroll isn't just writing a parable about growing up, though; he is playing with a number of questions of identity.

After Alice complains to the Caterpillar that her size has changed so much and that she is currently far too small, he tells her how to use the mushroom to grow larger or smaller at will. While learning to manage it, she inadvertently grows enormously tall, and alarms a Pigeon with her sinuous neck that bends among the tree branches. The Pigeon's belief that little girls must be a type of

serpent, since they eat eggs, is an amusing joke of logic, but it also causes Alice to question further her already-confused idea of her self. When the Pigeon adds, "You're looking for eggs, I know *that* well enough; and what does it matter to me whether you're a little girl or a serpent?" Alice answers, "It matters a great deal to *me*."

Once she is able to control her changes of size, Alice gains confidence and is less at the mercy of her circumstances. The Cheshire Cat is the next creature to call into question who Alice is, and he is unsuccessful. He offers the argument that everyone there is mad and so Alice must be mad, or she wouldn't have come

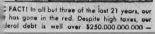

there. "Alice didn't think that proved it at all," and does not doubt her own sanity. This and the Cat's "proof" that he himself is mad, though, does invite the reader to wonder what defines madness and by what standards one could detect or prove insanity within one's own self.

In *Through the Looking-Glass*, examining the self is built right into the title. The adventure begins with the narrator telling us that Alice's favorite phrase is "Let's pretend," and that she likes to pretend to be other people. In this case, she pretends that the black kitten is the Red Queen, a device that ends the book as well. Making the kitten pose takes her to the mirror, and she wonders at length about the ways that the house in the mirror might be the same as and different from the real house. Having passed through the mirror, she learns that in fact the identity of what had been seen in the glass is different from what it had appeared to be. Alice is not confused over who she is, in the way that she was in her first adventure, but Looking-Glass Land contains a number of brain-teasers relating to identity.

In the fourth square of Alice's chess-board journey, the Gnat talks with her about names. She says she knows the names of some of the insects where she comes from:

"Of course they answer to their names?" the Gnat remarked carelessly. "I never knew them to do it." "What's the use of their having names, the Gnat said, "if they won't answer to them?" "No use to them," said Alice; "But it's useful to the people that name them, I suppose. If not, why do things have names at all?"

Indeed, even if little creatures do not care about their identity, we still want to be able to identify them. Alice and the Gnat proceed to discuss the names and characteristics of Looking-Glass insects, and then the Gnat, who mentioned that there lies ahead a wood where things have no names, imagines that it might be convenient not to be identified. If Alice had no name at home, the governess couldn't call her to lessons. The effect of having no name is soon to be tested, for Alice enters the wood—and suddenly she can't think of the name of anything. A Fawn comes by and, as neither of them has any idea who or what they are, it is possible for them to walk together, with Alice's arms "clasped lovingly round the soft neck of the Fawn." Once out in the open, "the Fawn gave a sudden bound into the air, and shook itself free from Alice's arms. 'I'm a Fawn!' it cried out in a voice of delight, 'and, dear me! you're a human child!'" It runs away in fright, leaving Alice ready to cry, and leaving the reader to consider the notion that knowing who and what we and our companions are determines our response to them. If the world were a wood with no names, would we all be able to walk, free of prejudice, arm in arm?

The characters Alice encounters next also raise problems of identity, for they are identical. Tweedledee and Tweedledum are distinguishable only because they have their names actually written on them. Their behavior is interchangeable and their image has become a staple in political cartooning, visual shorthand for two candidates who purport to offer a choice but who are really no different from each other.

Humpty Dumpty, who looks very like an egg but who objects to being mistaken for one, causes difficulties not only logical but also existential with his insistence on calling things whatever he chooses to call them. He first insists that a name must mean something: Alice's name is "stupid" because with it she could be almost any shape, whereas *his* name refers inherently to the shape of his body. However, while the rest of the world may be obliged to communicate with Humpty Dumpty in such meaningful terms, the reverse is not true: He uses words to mean whatever he chooses, and it is of no

import to him whether anyone can identify what he is referring to. Names may or may not create identity, but as Alice and the Gnat determine, they are useful to others. Humpty Dumpty dismisses Alice by raising another problem: To him, human faces are far too similar, and even though he and Alice have conversed, he will not be able to recognize her again. He might be able to tell her from other people if she had both eyes on the same side of her face, or her mouth on top, but as it is, her physical appearance is meaningless to him. Our faces are not who we are, of course, but they are an important part of human identity, and it's a chilling thought that someone might find our features, to us very personal and unique, indistinguishable from the faces of the rest of humanity.

What we mean when we try to talk about identity can be very confusing, and the language we have to work with doesn't help. Consider the following exchange between Alice and the White Knight:

"The name of the song is called 'Haddock's Eyes.'" "Oh, that's the name of the song, is it?" Alice said, trying to feel interested.

"No, you don't understand," the Knight said, looking a little vexed. "That's what the name is *called.* The name really is '*The Aged Aged Man.*'" "Then I ought to have said 'That's what the *song* is called'?" Alice corrected herself.

"No, you oughtn't: that's quite another thing! The *song* is called '*Ways and Means*': but that's only what it's *called,* you know!" "Well, what is the song, then?" said Alice, who was by this time completely bewildered.

"I was coming to that," the Knight said. The song really *is* '*A-sitting On a Gate.*'"

With the final banquet in her honor falling to pieces around her, Alice grabs the Red Queen and shakes her, and the Queen turns back into the black kitten as Alice wakes up. She immediately sets about identifying who the other cats had been in her dream, closing *Through the Looking-Glass* with concerns about who the characters really are. However, there is not a doubt about who Alice really is, as there had been in Wonderland, and when the characters challenge her she does not assume that she is no longer herself. When the Unicorn comes up to her, he is told excitedly:

"This is a child!.... We only found it to-day.
It's as large as life, and twice as natural!"
"I always thought they were
fabulous monsters!"
said the Unicorn. "Is it alive?"
"It can talk," said Haigha, solemnly.
The Unicorn looked dreamily at Alice, and said

"Talk, child."

Alice could not help her lips
curling up into a smile as she began:
"Do you know, I always thought
Unicorns were fabulous monsters, too!
I never saw one alive before!"
"Well, now that we have seen each other,"
said the Unicorn, "if you'll believe in me,
I'll believe in you."

Alice has no trouble believing in herself. She is equipped with the lessons she learned in Wonderland and with the Red Queen's parting advice from the beginning of the chess game: "Speak in French when you can't think of the English for a thing—turn out your toes as you walk—and remember who you are!"

Queen Alice

Alice's journey through Wonderland thus turns out to be an important voyage of self-discovery. Thrown into strange new circumstances, Alice has lost the normal framework of predictable events and conventional interactions that allows each of us to make it through the day without consciously thinking up all our speech and actions from scratch. Facing an unknown world without the aid of social conventions or even laws of nature to rely on, she has to manage on her own. She appreciates the immensity of this task, realizing immediately that all assumptions are open to question, as indicated early in the story when she is forced to go down to bedrock and question her assumptions about her own

Alice in the White Rabbit's House.

identity. Alice has a priceless opportunity to strip everything away and rebuild her comprehension of the world.

The first and main thing to be re-evaluated is conventional education. When Alice is falling down the rabbit hole, she believes that the things she has learned in her lessons will be of use to her in this predicament. "I wonder what Latitude and Longitude I've got to?" she muses. She prepares herself for the eventuality of falling right through the earth and of coming out in the "Antipathies," and even wonders about the etiquette of addressing the natives. Having been exposed to knowledge about the Antipodes has done her no good, even now when she might be able to use the information, nor has anything she might have known about natural science. She dozes off over the question **"Do cats eat bats?"** and is equally unable to answer the question **"Do bats eat cats?"**

None of these questions of geography or science is of the least use to her. Even if she could answer them, they prove to be irrelevant in her circumstances. In the Pool of Tears, she tries to make use of her knowledge of history and French in socializing with the Mouse, but none of her training prevents the interaction from being a total failure. Not only is academic information unreliable, but advice and practical instruction fail her, too. When she is evaluating the "Drink Me" bottle, she remembers the ample advice, received in moralizing tales, about how children can avoid injury and death. She is successful in not being poisoned, but in fact Carroll makes sure we get the joke that this is no thanks to her knowledge: She knows to not drink from a bottle marked "poison" but believes that since the bottle is not marked poison, it must therefore be safe. This is not only a logic joke and a death joke, it is also a rejection of reliance on received knowledge.

Abject and increasingly desperate about her identity, the enormously tall Alice sits in the pool of her own tears and tries to establish who she is. She chooses to do this by testing her knowledge. Reciting her multiplication tables and geography lessons does not work out well, and when she tries to recite Isaac Watts's upright little poem, "How Doth the Little Busy Bee," her voice betrays her and produces her own rather vicious "How Doth the Little Crocodile." Believing that her academic failure proves that she is no longer Alice, she decides to stay down the rabbit hole until she becomes someone she would like to be.

It is perhaps this point of crisis that frees Alice and allows her to stop relying on her education to interpret the world for her. She begins to show signs that she is trying a new tack—paying attention to what is going on around her and using her own mind to evaluate the situation. In the White Rabbit's house, she comes across another bottle of something, and although it has no "Drink Me" label, she chooses to drink it. "'I know *something* interesting is sure to happen,'" she said to herself, 'whenever I eat or drink anything; so I'll just see what this bottle does.'" Despite the fact that this results in her becoming so large that she completely fills the room and has to put a foot up the chimney, Alice does not regard the experiment as a total failure. Debating with herself on the desirability of the situation, she thinks, "I almost wish I hadn't gone down that rabbit hole—and yet—and yet—it's rather curious, you know, this sort of life!" Unable to regret her lack of prudence, Alice relishes her adventures, believing that there ought to be a book written about her, and thinks she will do it herself.

Alice continues to make attempts at coming to grips with her new circumstances. She begins to think that very few things are really impossible,

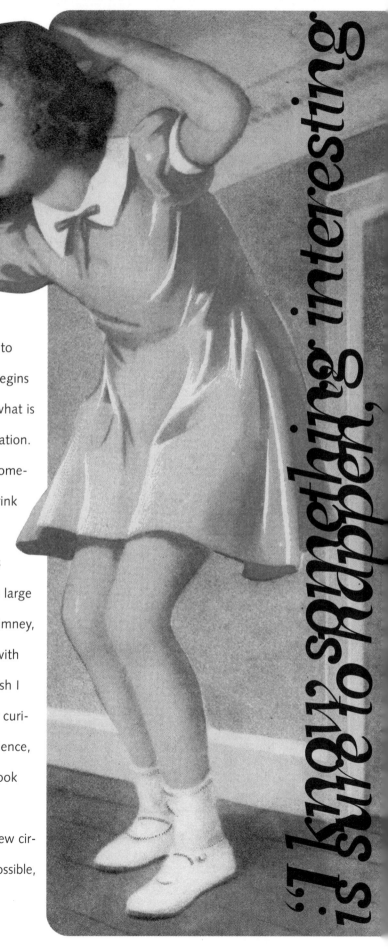

"I know something is sure to happen, interesting."

and early on finds it "quite dull and stupid for things to go on in the common way." She experiments with the mushroom pieces until she learns to control her size, and approaches the Duchess with some confidence. She has also absorbed the lesson that ordinary conversational rules no longer apply here, and is less thrown by the Duchess's rudeness, and even her order to have Alice beheaded, than she was by the Caterpillar's abruptness.

Chatting with the Duchess, Alice attempts to show off her education once more, but her explanation that it takes twenty-four hours for the earth to turn on its axis only proves to remind the Duchess of axes and beheading. Alice is willing to accept the baby's turning into a pig as scientifically inevitable, and, having learned about this phenomenon, wonders how she might duplicate the results with certain children of her acquaintance. Her open-mindedness about what is possible continues as she converses with the Cheshire Cat:

"You'll see me there," said the Cat, and vanished.

Alice was not much surprised at this, she was getting so well used to queer things happening. While she was still looking at the place where the suddenly appeared again.

"Bye-the-bye, what became of the baby?" said the Cat. "I'd nearly forgotten to ask."

"It turned into a pig," Alice answered very quietly, just as if the Cat had come back in a natural way.

"I thought it would," said the Cat, and vanished again.

Alice is not only able to be calm about the Cat's defiance of conventional physics, she is also unfazed by his conversational style. She does not believe everything he tells her, nor is she concerned about the unconventional structure of their conversation. This is an Alice with more inner resources than the child who had been reduced to tears by her growing and shrinking and who had felt helplessly frustrated by the Caterpillar's rudeness.

Alice's ability to respond to a situation that fits no formula and that defies structure is put to a trial by fire. She wanders into a tea party that never ends because one of the principals has offended Time and the clock is forever stopped at six. The participants have no stake in being pleasant to Alice and no interest in accommodating anyone's expectations. The Hatter complains that his watch is two days wrong and dips it in tea.

"What a funny watch!" she remarked. "It tells the day of the month, and doesn't tell what o'clock it is!"

"Why should it?" muttered the Hatter. "Does _your_ watch tell you what year it is?"

"Of course not," Alice replied very readily: "but that's because it stays the same year for such a long time together."

"Which is just the case with _mine_," said the Hatter.

Alice felt dreadfully puzzled. The Hatter's remark seemed to her to have no sort of meaning in it, and yet it was certainly English. "I don't quite understand you," she said, as politely as she could.

"The Dormouse is asleep again," said the Hatter, and he poured a little hot tea on to its nose.

Alice is puzzled for most of the conversation, but she is observant and manages to figure out how the tea party came to be never-ending and why as a result, so many tea things were on the table. She responds to some of the outrageous rudeness with some of her own, and if necessary chooses not to notice some remarks. She bravely continues to ask questions, which generally accomplish nothing other than to get her called "stupid" at one point. Alice finally has enough: Having made the effort to understand the situation, done her best to participate, and learned that it is not worth her while, she realizes there is no point in continuing. Alice no longer believes she has to learn and then play by the rules. Having sized up the situation, she does the sensible thing: She walks away.

Now that she is able to implement her knowledge of how things seem to work in Wonderland, Alice reaches her original goal of getting into the garden. Having decided not to copy the gardeners and to lie face down, she observes the royal procession and realizes that the monarchs of Wonderland are only playing cards. Alice, who had been afraid to cross the White Rabbit in the beginning of the book, does not feel at all obliged to tremble before Their Majesties:

"And who are these?" said the Queen, pointing to the three gardeners....
"How should I know?" said Alice, surprised at her own courage.
"It's no business of mine."
The Queen turned crimson with fury, and, after glaring at her
for a moment like a wild beast, began screaming, *"Off with her head! Off—"*
"Nonsense!"
said Alice, very loudly and decidedly, and the Queen was silent.

Finally, at the trial of the Knave of Hearts, Alice quickly sees how ludicrous the proceedings are. Simultaneously, she begins to return to her full size. She refuses to leave the courtroom and accuses the King of inventing Rule Forty-two on the spot ("*All persons over a mile high to leave the court*"), then argues with him over the validity of the evidence. Feeling firmly herself, full-sized and able to make her own decisions, Alice smashes the courtroom into nothingness in one of the most powerful moments in literature. All it takes to break the spell, the illusion that she is subject to their authority, is to speak the truth aloud:

"You're nothing but a pack of cards!"

Seldom have children been so empowered. Lewis Carroll was an entirely independent thinker. To him, it was a human right and duty to take nothing at face value, to think logically, and to discover the underlying truth in all things, great and small. To rely on conventions and ideologies was at best an abdication of one's humanity and at worst a grave error that left one susceptible to the sophistry of evil influences. Carroll made it one of his life's missions to educate people to think for themselves, and in Alice he has given children an extraordinary gift.

21

Throughout the book, Alice's assumptions about how to interact with other people fail her, as does her school-room education. As we have seen, she develops a canny eye for what is really happening around her. She stops relying on formulas and starts behaving in a genuine, unique manner. The Alice who tries to make conversation with mice and birds by chatting about cats and dogs comes a long way to become the Alice who can converse with the Cheshire Cat. The Alice who thinks she must obey the White Rabbit and fetch his gloves grows to be the Alice who talks back to the Queen of Hearts.

Scholars often comment on the aspect of *Alice's Adventures in Wonderland* that children have always loved about the book—its subversiveness. This charming and innocent-seeming story teaches children, and anyone else who cares to learn, a lesson that has toppled empires. Nothing is more dangerous to any kind of a system than members who can think for themselves. It's no wonder that the culture of the 1960s adopted Alice as a kind of mascot, a radical who questioned authority like no one else.

Lewis Carroll liked order and civilized behavior as much as anyone, and would not have welcomed a world in constant upheaval. However, he also knew that most people, far from being inclined to anarchy, are much too fond of the comfort that comes with surrendering their right to think, and often don't even know that they've surrendered it. His cry was for people to become fully human, to be kind to others as well as true to themselves. The narrative voice in the *Alice* books often praises Alice for the thoughtfulness and restraint in her dealings. As she grows in discernment and independence, Alice does not lose her politeness or sweet nature. Carroll himself was very like the person he has Alice become and who he invites us all to be: someone who is unfailingly civil, generous, and kind, and who also knows when to call a pack of cards a pack of cards.

Life What Is It But a Dream?

chapter eight

Alice's Adventures in Wonderland and *Through the Looking-Glass* thrive in our cultures and command our attention by means of an arsenal of hidden power sources—the imperious summons of the journey, the archetypal and haunting characters, the gripping and playful language, the tantalizing dark side, the mystery of our search for identity, and the glowing gift of personal autonomy. There is one more aspect of the *Alice* books that charges them with meaning: It is revealed at the end of both stories that they have been dreams. Alice has not actually traveled to magical fantasy lands, like Middle Earth or Narnia, she has journeyed within her own psyche.

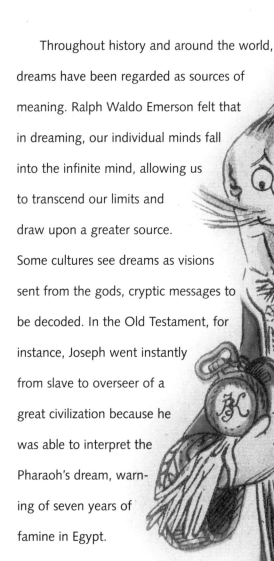

Throughout history and around the world, dreams have been regarded as sources of meaning. Ralph Waldo Emerson felt that in dreaming, our individual minds fall into the infinite mind, allowing us to transcend our limits and draw upon a greater source. Some cultures see dreams as visions sent from the gods, cryptic messages to be decoded. In the Old Testament, for instance, Joseph went instantly from slave to overseer of a great civilization because he was able to interpret the Pharaoh's dream, warning of seven years of famine in Egypt. Dreams can be so compelling, it is almost irresistible to believe them omens.

It is not just in ancient or primitive cultures that people have looked for someone who can interpret their dreams. Today in America, the Psychology and Self-Help sections of bookstores are filled with books that catalogue standard meanings of dream elements, and one can buy special dream diaries for recording and analyzing one's own dreams. We don't believe in the power of a priest or shaman to translate for us the message the gods have sent, but we do believe that our subconscious may be speaking to us in symbols that a Jungian psychoanalyst or some other counselor, chosen from a menu of theories ranging from Freudian to New Age, can help us read. These professionals tell us that dreams bring us the truth in a way that we are able to hear it. We may determinedly ignore what we do not wish to face, but dreams slip in under our radar, and drop their bombs on our defenseless sleeping minds.

Perhaps Carroll had unusual access to that great primordial reservoir that we call the subconscious when he "dreamed up" the stories. Certainly he began the original tale of Alice's adventures underground in dreamlike conditions. Idling in a gently rocking boat on a warm summer's afternoon, the sunlight sparkling on the water, with beloved children listening breathlessly, he leaned back and extemporaneously poured out his story, following his hunches as Alice followed the rabbit. It would be misleading to ignore that he also labored long and hard refining *Alice's Adventures in Wonderland* and piecing together *Through the Looking-Glass* from years of snippets and stories. However, it is essential to its being that *Alice* gushed forth from a talented storyteller at the peak of his abilities in ideal conditions, when he could relax and tap

into the richest vein of invention beneath his conscious control. Even when he was deliberately sculpting his tales, he seems to have had a tremendous ability to use his entire mind—right, left, conscious, unconscious—and to synthesize aspects of the human experience into a unity that speaks to the heart, mind, and spirit.

How successfully do the books evoke the aura of a dream? The straight-faced presentation of peculiar events resembles our unquestioning experience of bizarre circumstances when we are dreaming. Alice is surprised at first by her size-changes, but after that, she is not much disturbed by talking with a caterpillar or an egg. What's more, the narrative voice never marvels at what it is describing. At times it might get a twinkle in its eye, so to speak, but its matter-of-factness brings the strange creatures and their world solidly to life precisely because they are not questioned—just as in dreams it is not an issue whether to accept what is happening. One merely experiences the dream while it's unraveling, then contemplates it afterward.

The most dreamlike moments in the books may be the transitions where one scene melts away into another. Strange and wonderful beings and events belong to the waking imagination as well, but it is a particular characteristic of dreams that our surroundings shift, fade, and change into something else in a way that seems quite normal at the time. We are in the hall of doors when Alice's foot slips and she falls into the pool of her own giant-sized TEARS

and she swims about, meeting the Mouse as she looks for a way out of the salt water. At last she and the birds and animals crawl out onto the bank of the pool and spend some time onshore with the Caucus Race before she runs off to the White Rabbit's house. The hall of doors has vanished, to be reentered not by backtracking, but by a magical door in a tree.

The Old Sheep's shop transmogrifies in an especially beautiful way. Having come into being around her as the White Queen turns into the Sheep, the shop is full of fascinating items that Alice can't quite get a look at. She can see them out of the corner of her eye, like stars, but whenever she focuses on one, it eludes her. The shop then dissolves into a tranquil river where they glide in a rowboat among scented rushes. Alice rolls up her sleeves and gathers the lovely dream-rushes, but they quickly fade. The river dissolves back into the shop, which fades away behind her as she pursues an egg that turns out to be Humpty Dumpty.

One revealing connection to Alice on the theme of dreaming is the Australian aboriginal concept of the Dreamtime. When *Alice's Adventures in Wonderland* was translated into Pitjantjatjara in 1975, under the auspices of the University of Adelaide, it became *Alitji in the Dreamtime*. No doubt Alice was right at home, for the similarities are startling. The Dreamtime, simply put, is an eternal past, populated by beings who are simultaneously ancestors and archetypes. Living people can enter the Dreamtime while asleep and learn life lessons from those beings. Waking from their journey as if from a vision, they bring the lessons with them. Wonderland, too, seems to be a land of eternally cyclic events, played out by characters that typify different human possibilities. It becomes accessible to Alice in her dream, and there she learns valuable lessons about how to live a more fully realized life. No one suggests that this was deliberate on Carroll's part, but it adds to the richness of *Alice* to see another culture make use of dreaming in such a resonant and similar way.

Scholarly essays abound discussing the meaning of Alice's trips through Wonderland and Looking-Glass Land. Is she aggressively bursting in on the characters' lives, rudely arguing with one and all? Is she representative of the British Empire, blindly applying her standards to a New World? Perhaps she is a Parsival figure, questing in a strange land populated by characters who are deliberately difficult in order to foil her. Is she more sinning or sinned against? Part of the richness of the books is their capacity to support so many interpretations. Unlike a more pat fable, neither story is ever exhausted.

A critical approach that begins with the assumption that both stories are dreams, however, sends the inquiry in a new direction. In this vein, Alice cannot be criticized for her behavior, because she is not in a real social situation. She is inside her own head, interacting with pieces of herself. The characters must be considered as parts of Alice and of her perception of the world, and the situations become events she needs to experience. Tumbling down the rabbit hole, she falls into her subconscious, and then in the second book, she passes through her own reflection into herself, both powerful images of going inward. And

what does she find there? Anxiety about growing up, hostile and contentious parts of herself, conflicts with authority, life as a game to be deciphered and won, love that is only partly effective in protecting her, and the inner strength and self-reliance to take control of her life. She sees madness, and rejects it for order and sanity; she sees mystery and death, and absorbs them as part of life.

In the final moments of the stories, Alice's waking up reveals to us that her magical adventures were not "real." Children are sometimes disappointed by this, and feel cheated to learn that they had not accompanied Alice to a *real* fantasy world. Indeed, Wonderland is not a place we, too, can stumble across, in the way that many lovers of fantasy literature nurse a small secret hope that they will someday open a closet and find a door to Narnia. Yet, as we grow older, we can appreciate better just how real the *Alice* books are: Being dreams, they *are* Alice. As for us, Carroll has given us the knowledge that we all contain and embody marvelous worlds, that within each of us is a Wonderland.

Lewis Carroll brings the conundrum of the reality of dreams to our attention overtly in *Through the Looking-Glass.* Tweedledum and Tweedledee take Alice to see the Red King asleep under a tree in his night-cap, snoring like steam-engine. Tweedledee glee-fully tells Alice that the King is dreaming about her, and asks where she supposes she'd be if he left off.

"Where I am now, of course," said Alice. "Not you!" Tweedledee retorted contemptu-ously. "You'd be nowhere. Why, you're only a sort of thing in his dream!"

"If that there King was to wake," added Tweedledum, "you'd go out—bang!—just like a candle!"

"I shouldn't!" Alice exclaimed indignantly. "Besides, if I'm only a sort of thing in his dream, what are *you,* I should like to know!"

"Ditto," said Tweedledum.

"Ditto, ditto!" cried Tweedledee.

He shouted this so loud that Alice couldn't help saying, "Hush! You'll be waking him, I'm afraid, if you make *so* much noise."

"Well, it's no use *your* talking about waking him," said Tweedledum, "when you're only one of the things in his dream. You know very well you're not real."

"I *am* real!" said Alice, and began to cry.

Later on, when the scene with the Lion and the Unicorn disappears in a terrible drumming, Alice wonders if she had dreamed it, and sees that she hadn't, for the plum-cake dish is still there:

"So I wasn't dreaming, after all," she said to herself, "unless—unless we're all part of the *same* dream. Only I *do* hope it's *my* dream, and not the Red King's! I don't like belonging to another person's dream," she went on in a rather com-plaining tone: "I've a good mind to go and wake him, and *see* what happens!"

So I wasn't dreaming, after all, she said to herself, 'unless—unless we're all part of the same dream. Only I *do* hope it's *my* dream, and not the Red King's! I don't like belonging to another person's dream," she went on in a rather complaining tone: "I've a good mind to go and wake him, and see what happens!"

When she has finally shaken the Red Queen back into a kitten and wakes up in her chair by the fire, the story ends with Alice beseeching the kitten to help her consider who dreamed it, and then the narrative voice asks the reader "Which do *you* think it was?" Surely it was Alice, and still—and still—what if we are all part of someone's, maybe God's, dream? How would we know? And what if God wakes up? Dreams are so real while they are happening and contain so much truth, while life itself is strange and fleeting.

Carroll closes the second book with a haunting little poem, an acrostic on the full name of the real Alice. It harkens back to the golden afternoon on the river when the story began, and longs for a kind of Dreamtime, an eternal past where Alice always lives and where children yet unborn dream away the time until they will nestle near a storyteller and hear the timeless tale of Alice, which is everyone's story. The poem ends,

Ever drifting down the stream—
Lingering in the golden gleam—
Life, what is it but a dream?

Frontis: "The poor little Lizard, Bill, was in the middle," by Harry Rountree, from *Alice's Adventures in Wonderland and Through the Looking-Glass* (London: Collins' Clear-Type Press, 1928). **Page 4:** Alice peering through the little door at the beautiful garden, by Jourcin, from *Alice au pays des merveilles* (Alice in Wonderland) translated by R. and A. Prophétie (Paris: Editions G.P., 1948) **Page 5:** The Owl and the Panther, by Greg Hildebrandt, from *Alice in Wonderland* (New Jersey: The Unicorn Publishing House, 1990).

A Story, the Truth, and a True Story.
Pages 8–9: The Cook, Alice, and the Duchess in the kitchen, by Jourcin, from *Alice au pays des merveilles* (Alice in Wonderland) translated by R. and A. Prophétie (Paris: Editions G.P., 1948). **Page 10:** (*top*) Cover of a Russian edition, *Anya v Stranye Chudes* (Anya in Wonderland), illustrated by S. Zalshypin, translated by Vladimir Nabokov (Berlin: Izdatel'stuo Ganayun, 1923); (*bottom*) From a brochure advertising Congressional Documents on Demand of Bethesda, MD, ca. 1989. **Page 11:** Alice first sees the White Rabbit, by Frank Adams, from *Alice's Adventures in Wonderland* (London: Blackie & Son Ltd., 1912). **Page 12:** Self-portrait by Lewis Carroll. **Pages 12–13:** (*background*) Signature of C.L. Dodgson. **Page 13:** Stone placed in honor of Lewis Carroll in Poets' Corner, Westminster Abbey, London. **Pages 14–15:** Lewis Carroll with the children of fantasy writer George MacDonald. **Page 16:** Alice with jurors, by Germaine Bouret, from *Alice au pays des merveilles* (Alice in Wonderland, Monte Carlo: Editions "Les Flots Bleus," 1951). **Page 17:** Alice with the Dodo and other Pool of Tears characters, illustrator not credited, from *Alice in Wonderland* fold-out book (England: Raphael Tuck & Sons, Ltd., n.d.). **Page 18:** (*top*) Partial pieces from The Mad Tea-Party Puzzle, Made in England by J. Salmon, Ltd., Sevenoaks; (*center: left to right*) Guinness advertisement featuring the Queen of Hearts; Yellowstone National Park brochure "Alice's Adventures in the New Wonderland"; From an article in *The American Weekly*, pp. 16–17 (11 August 1946) about

Disney's *Alice in Wonderland*, showing versions of the characters that were not used in the final film; (*bottom left*) "Alice's Race in Wonderland" board game, manufactured by H.P. Gibson and Sons, Ltd.; (*bottom right*) "Adventures of Alice in Wonderland Game," manufactured by Milton Bradley Company, Springfield, MA, as a tie-in to the 1933 Paramount film starring Charlotte Henry. **Page 19:** Sheet music for "Alice in Wonderland Fox-Trot for Orchestra," by Charlie Tobias, Jack Schroll, and Murray Mencher. (New York: Leo Feist, 1933). **Page 20:** (*top*) The Gryphon asleep, drawn by Lewis Carroll, from *Alice's Adventures under Ground*, (London: Macmillan, 1886); (*bottom*) Alice and the Red Queen running, by John Tenniel, from *Through the Looking-Glass and What Alice Found There* (London: Macmillan, 1872). **Page 21:** The Gryphon asleep, by John Tenniel, from *Alice's Adventures in Wonderland* (London: Macmillan, 1866). **Page 22:** Alice about to follow the White Rabbit down the rabbit hole, by A.L. Bowley, from *Alice in Wonderland* (London: Raphael Tuck & Sons, 1921). **Page 23:** Alice and the White Knight, by John Tenniel, from *Through the Looking-Glass* (London: Macmillan, 1872).

There and Back Again
Pages 24–25: Alice falling down the rabbit hole, by Greg Hildebrandt, from *Alice in Wonderland* (New Jersey: The Unicorn Publishing House, 1990). **Page 26:** The Gryphon leading Alice to the trial, illustrator not credited, from *Alice in Wonderland* (London: Juvenile Productions Ltd., n.d.). **Page 27:** Alice falling down the rabbit hole, by Blanche McManus, from *Alice's Adventures in Wonderland and Through the Looking-Glass* (New York: The Platt & Peck Co., 1900). **Page 28:** The Hatter shaking out of his shoes at the trial, by Jourcin, from *Alice au pays des merveilles* (Alice in Wonderland) translated by R. and A. Prophétie (Paris: Editions G.P., 1948). **Page 29:** (*top*) Alice about to go through the looking-glass, by John Tenniel, from *Through the Looking-Glass* (London: Macmillan, 1872); (*center*) from the Hatter shaking out of his shoes at the trial, by Jourcin, from *Alice au pays des merveilles* (Alice in Wonderland) translated by R.

and A. Prophétie (Paris: Editions G.P., 1948); (*bottom*) Alice pulling back curtain, by John Tenniel, from *Alice's Adventures in Wonderland* (London: Macmillan, 1866). **Page 30:** (*left*) Alice and the Caterpillar on the cover of *Alice in Wonderland 3 Way Tracing, Puzzle & Story Book* (London: Bairns Books, Ltd., n.d.); (*right*) the White Rabbit checking his watch, by John Tenniel, from *Alice's Adventures in Wonderland* (London: Macmillan, 1866). **Page 31:** Alice watching the Red Queen hammer in a peg marker, by Blanche McManus, from *Alice's Adventures in Wonderland and Through the Looking-Glass* (New York: The Platt & Peck Co., 1900). **Page 32:** The Card Gardeners painting the roses red, by Henry Morin, from *Alice au pays des merveilles et de l'autre côté du miroir* (Alice in Wonderland and Through the Looking-Glass), translated by M.-M. Fayet (Paris: Nelson, Éditeurs, 1939). **Page 33:** The Gryphon, Alice, and the Mock Turtle, by A. Rado, from *Alice's Adventures in Wonderland* (London: W.H. Cornelius, 1944). **Pages 34–35:** Alice and the Cheshire Cat, by Greg Hildebrandt, from *Alice in Wonderland* (New Jersey: The Unicorn Publishing House, 1990).

Figures of Fun
Pages 36–37: Alice looking at the Caterpillar, by Gwynedd M. Hudson, from *Alice's Adventures in Wonderland* (London: Boots the Chemist/Hodder and Stoughton, 1922). **Page 38:** Giant Alice at the outdoor trial, by Henry Morin, from *Alice au pays des merveilles et de l'autre côté du miroir* (Alice in Wonderland and Through the Looking-Glass), translated by M.-M. Fayet (Paris: Nelson, Éditeurs, 1939). **Page 39:** (*left*) The Cook, Alice, and the Duchess in the kitchen, by W.H. Walker, from *Alice's Adventures in Wonderland* (London: John Land The Bodley Head Ltd., 1907); (*right*) the Red Queen propping Alice against a tree, by M.L. Kirk, from *Through the Looking-Glass* (New York: Frederick A. Stokes Company, 1905). **Page 40:** The Mouse's Tale, by Figueiredo Sobral, from *Alice no país das maravilhas* (Alice in Wonderland), translated by Maria de Meneses (Lisbon: Portugália Editora, n.d.). **Page 41:** Alice accepting a thimble from the Dodo, by John Tenniel, from *The Nursery Alice,* by

Lewis Carroll, illustrated and colored by John Tenniel (London: Macmillan, 1889). **Page 42:** Alice walking away from the Mad Tea-party, by Frank Adams, from *Alice's Adventures in Wonderland* (London: Blackie & Son Ltd., 1912). **Page 43:** The Duchess and Alice walking at the croquet game, by Gordon Robinson, from *Alice's Adventures in Wonderland* (New York: Sam'l Gabriel Sons & Company, 1916). **Page 44:** The croquet game, by A. Rado, from *Alice's Adventures in Wonderland* (London: W.H. Cornelius, 1944). **Page 46:** Alice shaking hands with Humpty Dumpty, by John Tenniel, from *Through the Looking-Glass* (London: Macmillan, 1872). **Page 47:** Tweedledee and Tweedledum salt-and-pepper shakers, ca. 1980s.

Webs of Words
Pages 48–49: Trial scene, by Gwynedd M. Hudson, from *Alice's Adventures in Wonderland* (London: Boots the Chemist/Hodder and Stoughton, 1922). **Page 51:** Alice and the Caterpillar, by Jourcin, from *Alice au pays des merveilles* (Alice in Wonderland) translated by R. and A. Prophétie (Paris: Editions G.P., 1948). **Page 52:** Queen Alice at the door with the Frog, by René Cloke, from *Through the Looking-Glass* (London: P.R. Gawthorne, Ltd., 1950). **Page 53:** (*top*) The Cheshire Cat disappearing, by Blanche McManus, from *Alice's Adventures in Wonderland and Through the Looking-Glass* (New York: The Platt & Peck Co., 1900); (*bottom*) the White King making a memorandum, by Harry Rountree, from *Alice's Adventures in Wonderland and Through the Looking-Glass* (London: Collins' Clear-Type Press, 1928). **Pages 54–55:** Humpty Dumpty and Alice, by Blanche McManus, from *Alice's Adventures in Wonderland and Through the Looking-Glass* (New York: The Platt & Peck Co., 1900). **Page 56:** The Cheshire Cat and Alice, by Wiltraud Jasper, from *Alice im Wunderland* (Alice in Wonderland), translated by Kurt Schrey (Oplanden: Verlag Friedrich Middelhauve, 1958). **Page 57:** Long-necked Alice with the Pigeon, illustrator not credited, from cartoon-style Japanese edition. **Page 58:** The Hatter, Dormouse, March Hare, and Alice on sleeve of record album from Peter Pan records, 1950. **Page 59:** Alice with the Gryphon and Mock Turtle, by

Gwynedd M. Hudson, from *Alice's Adventures in Wonderland* (London: Boots the Chemist/Hodder and Stoughton, 1922). **Pages 60–61:** Alice grown large at the trial, illustrator not credited, from *Alice in Wonderland* (London: Juvenile Productions Ltd., n.d.). **Page 62:** Psychedelic poster of the Mad Tea-party. **Page 63:** The Hatter, by John Tenniel, from *Alice's Adventures in Wonderland* (London: Macmillan, 1866). **Page 64:** Alice leaving the Mad Tea-party, by Wiltraud Jasper, from *Alice im Wunderland* (Alice in Wonderland), translated by Kurt Schrey (Oplanden: Verlag Friedrich Middelhauve, 1958). **Page 65:** Alice at the banquet, seated between the Red and White Queens, by Blanche McManus, from *Alice's Adventures in Wonderland and Through the Looking-Glass* (New York: The Platt & Peck Co., 1900).

The Tulgey Wood
Pages 66–67: Alice towering over the Duchess's house, by Uriel Birnbaum, from *Alice im Spiegelland* (Alice in Wonderland), translated by Helene Schen-Riesz (Vienna: Sesam—Verlag, 1923). **Page 68:** Alice looking at mushroom cloud, on the front cover of *Alice's Adventures in Atomland in the Plastic Age,* by Richard Field (South Duxbury, MA: Faulkner and Field, 1949). **Page 69:** Alice on the cover of theater program for the play, *Alice,* Omnibus Theater Co., Montreal. **Page 70:** Alice falling down the rabbit hole, by M.L. Kirk, from *Alice's Adventures in Wonderland* (New York: Frederick A. Stokes Company, 1904). **Page 71:** Alice about to enter the door in the tree, by Greg Hildebrandt, from *Alice in Wonderland* (New Jersey: The Unicorn Publishing House, 1990). **Page 72:** Alice grown huge inside White Rabbit's house, drawn by Lewis Carroll, from *Alice's Adventures under Ground,* (London: Macmillan, 1886). **Page 73:** The Caucus Race, by Blanche McManus, from *Alice's Adventures in Wonderland and Through the Looking-Glass* (New York: The Platt & Peck Co., 1900). **Page 74:** Alice in the Duchess's kitchen, by Gordon Robinson, from *Alice's Adventures in Wonderland* (New York: Sam'l Gabriel Sons & Company, 1916). **Page 75:** Slithy toves, mome raths, and borgoves, by Uriel Birnbaum, from *Alice im Spiegelland* (Alice in Wonderland),

translated by Helene Schen-Riesz (Vienna: Sesam—Verlag, 1923). **Page 76:** (*background*) The Jabberwock, by John Tenniel, from *Through the Looking-Glass* (London: Macmillan, 1872); (*foreground*) The Jabberwock, by Harry Rountree, from *Alice's Adventures in Wonderland and Through the Looking-Glass* (London: Collins' Clear-Type Press, 1928). **Page 77:** (*background*) From The Jabberwock, by John Tenniel, from *Through the Looking-Glass* (London: Macmillan, 1872); (*right*) Alice and Humpty Dumpty, by Bessie Pease Gutmann, from *Through the Looking-Glass and What Alice Found There* (New York: Dodge Publishing Company, 1909). **Pages 78–79:** Alice and the Red Queen running, by Bessie Pease Gutmann, from *Through the Looking-Glass and What Alice Found There* (New York: Dodge Publishing Company, 1909). **Page 80:** Alice meeting the White Rabbit, by Arthur Rackham, from *Alice's Adventures in Wonderland* (London: William Heinemann; New York: Doubleday, Page & Company, 1907). **Page 81:** The Knave of Hearts from the front cover of *Alice in Wonderland: A Play,* by Emily Prime Delafield (New York: Dodd, Mead & Company, 1898). **Page 82:** The banquet goes haywire, by Bessie Pease Gutmann, from *Through the Looking-Glass and What Alice Found There* (New York: Dodge Publishing Company, 1909). **Page 83:** The banquet goes haywire, by Uriel Birnbaum, from *Alice im Spiegelland* (Alice in Wonderland), translated by Helene Schen-Riesz (Vienna: Sesam—Verlag, 1923).

Who Are You?
Pages 84–85: Alice shrinking from the Drink Me bottle, illustrator not credited, from cartoon-style Japanese edition. **Page 86:** Alice taking the key off the glass table, by Uriel Birnbaum, from *Alice im Spiegelland* (Alice in Wonderland), translated by Helene Schen-Riesz (Vienna: Sesam—Verlag, 1923). **Page 88:** Alice with the Caterpillar, by Figueiredo Sobral, from *Alice no país das maravilhas* (Alice in Wonderland), translated by Maria de Meneses (Lisbon: Portugália Editora, n.d.). **Page 89:** The upside-down woman in Australia or New Zealand, by Charles Robinson, from *Alice's Adventures in Wonderland*

(London: Cassell and Company, Ltd., 1907). **Page 90:** Tall Alice, by John Tenniel, from *The Nursery Alice,* by Lewis Carroll, illustrated and colored by John Tenniel (London: Macmillan, 1889). **Page 91:** (*full-color panel at top right*) From advertising comic book, "Alice in Wonderland: A Souvenir Tour of Your Wonder Bakery" (NY: Continental Baking Co., 1969); (*full-color panel at bottom left*) from "Alice in Blunderland," a comic book satire on government waste (New York: Industrial Services, 1952). **Page 92:** Alice asleep on the cover of *The Nursery Alice,* by Lewis Carroll, with cover illustration by E. Gertrude Thomson (London: Macmillan, 1889). **Page 93:** Magazine ad for Philco refrigerators. **Page 94:** Alice turning away from the Caterpillar, by W.H. Walker, from *Alice's Adventures in Wonderland* (London: John Land The Bodley Head Ltd., 1907). **Page 95:** The Tweedles hide from the monstrous crow, by Henry Morin, from *Alice au pays des merveilles et de l'autre côté du miroir* (Alice in Wonderland and Through the Looking-Glass), translated by M.-M. Fayet (Paris: Nelson, Éditeurs, 1939). **Page 96:** Alice with upside-down White Knight, by M.L. Kirk, from *Through the Looking-Glass* (New York: Frederick A. Stokes Company, 1905). **Page 98:** The Lion and the Unicorn fighting, by Harry Rountree, from *Alice's Adventures in Wonderland and Through the Looking-Glass* (London: Collins' Clear-Type Press, 1928). **Pages 98–99:** Alice and the Red Queen in the garden, by René Cloke, from *Through the Looking-Glass* (London: P.R. Gawthorne, Ltd., 1950).

Queen Alice
Pages 100–101: Alice between the sleeping Red and White Queens, by Henry Morin, from *Alice au pays des merveilles et de l'autre côté du miroir* (Alice in Wonderland and Through the Looking-Glass), translated by M.-M. Fayet (Paris: Nelson, Éditeurs, 1939). **Page 102:** The White Rabbit in front of his house, illustrator not credited, from *Alice in Wonderland* fold-out book (England: Raphael Tuck & Sons, Ltd., n.d.). **Page 103:** Alice grown large from Eat Me cake, illustrator not credited, from *Alice in Wonderland* (London: Juvenile Productions Ltd., nd). **Page 104:** (*top*) Alice looking at the Cheshire Cat, by

John Tenniel, from *The Nursery Alice,* by Lewis Carroll, illustrated and colored by John Tenniel (London: Macmillan, 1889); (*bottom*) Alice with the pig baby and the Cheshire Cat, by Germaine Bouret, from *Alice au pays des merveilles* (Alice in Wonderland, Monte Carlo: Editions "Les Flots Bleus," 1951). **Page 105:** Mad Tea-party scene, illustrator not credited. **Page 106:** Alice hitting the ceiling in the courtroom, illustrator not credited, from a cartoon-style Japanese edition. **Page 108:** Alice at the Mad Tea-party, by John Tenniel, from *The Nursery Alice,* by Lewis Carroll, illustrated and colored by John Tenniel (London: Macmillan, 1889. **Page 109:** The Queen of Hearts and the Card Gardeners, by Frank Adams, from *Alice's Adventures in Wonderland* (London: Blackie & Son Ltd., 1912). **Pages 110–111:** Alice hitting the ceiling in the courtroom, illustrator not credited, from cartoon-style Japanese edition. **Page 112:** Alice holding flamingo, by Greg Hildebrandt, from *Alice in Wonderland* (New Jersey: The Unicorn Publishing House, 1990). **Page 113:** Alice fending off a shower of cards, by John Tenniel, from *The Nursery Alice,* by Lewis Carroll, illustrated and colored by John Tenniel (London: Macmillan, 1889.

Life, What Is It But a Dream?
Pages 114–115: Alice picking rushes in the Old Sheep's boat, by René Cloke, from *Through the Looking-Glass* (London: P.R. Gawthorne, Ltd., 1950). **Page 116:** The White Rabbit running, by Olga Siemaszko, from *Alicja W Krainie Czarów* (Alice in Wonderland), translated by Antoni Marianowicz (Warsaw: Nasza Ksiégarnia, 1955). **Page 117:** Alice with the Caterpillar, by A. Rado, from *Alice's Adventures in Wonderland* (London: W.H. Cornelius, 1944). **Page 118:** The Pool of Tears, by Olga Siemaszko, from *Alicja W Krainie Czarów* (Alice in Wonderland), translated by Antoni Marianowicz (Warsaw: Nasza Ksiégarnia, 1955). **Page 119:** Alice in the Old Sheep's shop, by M.L. Kirk, from *Through the Looking-Glass* (New York: Frederick A. Stokes Company, 1905). **Page 120:** Humpty Dumpty on the wall, by Uriel Birnbaum, from *Alice im Spiegelland* (Alice in Wonderland), translated by Helene Schen-Riesz (Vienna: Sesam—Verlag, 1923). **Page 121:** Alice with the talking flowers,